Amole Again

Amole Again

Gene Amole

SCRIPPS HOWARD

DENVER PUBLISHING COMPANY   1985

International Standard Book Number: 0-914807-03-X
Library of Congress Catalog Card Number: 85-072653
Copyright © 1985 by Gene Amole.
All rights reserved.
Printed in the United States of America.

Cover photograph by David L. Cornwell
Cover design by Ed Stein
Book design by Brad Thompson

First printing September 1985

To Mom

Also by Gene Amole

Morning

Contents

4. Time & time again

5. Reasons for seasons

6. Sauces and other spicy stuff

7. High-tech talk

Introduction

BOOKS OF NEWSPAPER COLUMNS ARE SOMETIMES CALLED "ANTHOLOGIES" or "collections." Whatever term is used to dignify them, such works are really double-dipping of the most obvious kind. After all, the columnist has already been paid once for writing them, and when the book comes out, he picks up a few more bucks for gilding the lily.

I figured that if you bought all the copies of the Rocky Mountain News to get the columns in my first book, "Morning," the cost would have been $31.50. Since "Morning" was priced at only $7.95, its readers got a real bargain. I always try to take a positive position on these matters.

While the idea behind "Amole Again" is much the same as for "Morning," there are some differences. Sure, I am still fascinated with the human condition, meatballs, nostalgia, bureaucratic double-speak, coping with high technology, family relationships and, of course, "October's bright blue weather." Those things are my stock in trade.

But in "Amole Again," I decided to touch on war, a subject about which I have rarely written. I was a soldier during World War II and a civilian correspondent with United Nations forces during the Korean War. I went to Korea in the belief that the story of the fighting man has never really been told accurately. I was going to be the guy to do it, or so I thought.

Actually, I wasn't any better at it than those who preceded me. There is something about confronting "the great death" in wartime that is almost impossible to translate into newspaper copy. But I gave it a shot anyhow.

I have included in "Amole Again" a couple of things I wrote during that period. I have always been distressed because the sacrifices of our soldiers, sailors and Marines in Korea have been overlooked. The Korean War is remembered now only because of the television series "M*A*S*H," a program that played that ugly little war mostly for laughs. To try to set the record straight, I have included a radio piece I wrote in 1951 which I now call "The real M*A*S*H."

I sincerely enjoyed writing the V-E Day story that ends the book. It resulted from a conversation I had with Joe Garner, a reporter at the

News. Knowing I had fought during World War II, he asked me one day why I hadn't done columns about D-day, the Battle of the Bulge, discovery of the death camps and the other 40th anniversary events recalled during 1984 and 1985. I told him I had been trying for 40 years to forget those things.

Then we talked about my experiences during the days that led up to V-E Day. "Why don't you write about that?" he asked. The more I thought about it, the better I liked Joe's idea. It was a story not about war, but about peace; not about hate, but about love.

In picking through old letters, photographs and mementos, and in reconstructing the events in my mind, a strange thing happened: I began to feel as though I were young again. And as I wrote, those events seemed to be in the present, not in the past of four decades ago. It was almost as though I had found a way to journey through the years and return to live again in another time.

Since the story was published, many readers have written to ask if I have since heard from Dorothy. I have not. I still don't know where she is. But we decided to try to find her. The News contacted The Mercury, the only newspaper in Hobart, Tasmania. Ross Gaeds, an editor there, told us he would try to find her. So far, though, he has been unable to do so. He is still trying.

Naturally, I would like to hear from her. That failing, I hope somehow she will read what I have written about that great moment in world history and in our lives. Maybe in this book, my story will somehow find its way to her. I hope so.

Again I want to thank the Rocky Mountain News and its editor, Ralph Looney, for the opportunity to publish this book. I also want to thank Brad Thompson for his invaluable editorial assistance; Ed Stein for his cover design; David Cornwell for the cover photograph; Zoe Lappin and Suzanne Weiss for having the patience to proofread my copy; and Chris Power for handling the business end of publishing this book.

1

NETWORKING

Initiating interface

"May I have your attention? Please. Good morning. I am your chairperson, and I want to welcome all of you. You'll agree that your splendid turnout certainly justifies the need for this seminar.

"As you will note from your program, we are here to develop action strategies. It isn't enough in these times to concern ourselves only with an overview of value clarifications. This is going to be a hands-on workshop, and we expect to accomplish a great deal.

"Workstylewise, we are going to be very much concerned with experiential and values clarification approaches. This is not to say that we won't touch on self-esteem and communication goals. There will be a general overview of this relationship.

"In the process of initiating and implementing guidelines, we shall concentrate on defining problem areas in inner game management settings. We'll have resource persons, and feedback is encouraged.

"No preceptorship training is complete without a clear understanding of role changes, social skills and interpersonal relations. This is no place for misinformation and flawed decision making.

"This session will be so structured as to embrace a system of intervention tactics. There will be an opportunity for group utilization during encounter environment sessions later.

"We shall be striking a balance between theoretical issues and down-to-earth policies. All the while, you will note, we are going to move toward the acceptance of change and growth as a social reality.

"As we move into program development, we'll be touching on survival methodologies and the management of stress. Each of us will be given the opportunity to design, implement and evaluate.

"If past experience is any indication, one of the most insightful sections of this seminar is our update on attitudinal dysfunction. Don't miss it. It will immediately follow the distress clinic.

"In order to access germane ideologies, we're going to have to interface our matching expectations with an objective performance appraisal. Don't hesitate to implement external proctoring if it is justified.

"Much of the afternoon session will be devoted to the consequences of confused priorities. We shall examine pre-emptive intervention and the need for reorientation.

"No meeting of this kind would be complete without some mention of viable alternatives and orchestrated processes. This does not mean we shall become mired in issue avoidance and decision postponement. No ambiguities, please. And plenty of input.

"You will note on your content outline that a discussion entitled 'Pathways to Overorganization' had been scheduled. It has been canceled and replaced by a clinic entitled 'Assessing Needs for Optimum Lifestyle Priorities.'

"If there is time, we shall try to put together a short skull session on isolating in on the philosophical fragmentations of the under-achiever. This will be covered when we break up in smaller groups.

"At this point in time, we have found that time management is the key to professional effectiveness. The definition and characteristics of assertive, non-assertive communications will be explained both in theory and in actual interpersonal relationships.

"That's about it. By maximizing our efforts, we'll be able to finalize and terminate this module on time, and we shall effect closure by 5 p.m. It should be an impactful experience. We'll be getting started shortly.

"Just as soon as we get organized."

February 8, 1981

Learn buzzspeak and wow 'em all

BUZZPHRASE.

University of Denver publicist Bud Mayer was cleaning his desk when he came up with an invaluable aid for speech writers, public relations directors and bureaucrats. It was given to him by Tom Goodale, a DU vice chancellor.

Skillfully used, the Buzzphrase Generator will permit you to "baffle your friends and amaze reporters with your lack of clarity." It will also help in the writing of speeches guaranteed to put listeners to sleep."

"Below you will find the Buzzphrase Generator, a new language machine favored by bureaucrats, educators, politicians and a rare breed of K mart managers. It consists of three paragraphs of buzzwords, each numbered zero to nine."

• (0) integrated. (1) total. (2) systematized. (3) parallel. (4) functional. (5) responsive. (6) optical. (7) synchronized. (8) compatible. (9) balanced.

• (0) management. (1) organizational. (2) monitored. (3) reciprocal. (4) digital. (5) logic. (6) transitional. (7) incremental. (8) third-generation. (9) policy.

• (0) options. (1) flexibility. (2) capability. (3) mobility. (4) programming. (5) concept. (6) timephase. (7) projection. (8) hardware. (9) contingency.

The Buzzword Generator is simplicity itself. That's the beauty of it. The smallest of minds can master it in moments. An infinite number of monkeys with a like number of Buzzword Generators would ultimately duplicate every government directive ever written.

Ready, class? OK, here's how it works. Think of any three-digit number. Doesn't matter what it is. Gov. Richard D. Lamm lives at 400 E. Eighth Ave. Let's run 400 through our Buzzword Generator to see what happens.

We take (4) from the first paragraph, (0) from the second and (0) from the third. And what do we get? "Functional management options." Isn't that beautiful? Lamm should certainly be able to work that into his next squabble with the Legislature over its usurping gubernational powers.

Mayor William H. McNichols Jr. lives at 745 Krameria St. Translated by our little, handy-dandy Buzzword Generator, we get "synchronized digital concept." Piece of cake for hizzoner to incorporate that in any explanation of shortfalls in Stapleton International Airport parking fees.

The Regional Transportation District headquarters is at 1600 Blake St. We take the first three digits for Buzzword Generator translation. Wow! The RTD is going to really love this. What we have, bureaucrats, is "total transitional options."

If the RTD hasn't used that one in its quarterly status report on the 16th Street Transitway/Mall, you can bet your buttons it will.

The originator of the Buzzword Generator is not known. It is believed to be Alexander Haig, however. He certainly had a flair for bureaucratese, or "Haigspeak," as it was called. I always liked Haig's "Let me context that for you," and his classic "I want to caveat that." He mixed nouns and verbs as effortlessly as he stirred a martini.

He was also a master of 131.

August 19, 1982

Yes, have a nice day

PROCLAMATION.

It is about time for my annual "have a nice day" column. I was reminded of this when a physician friend commented the other day that he always considered the expression to be trite.

I have been a lone defender of "have a nice day" since the beginning. I have always liked it because it does convey a sense of friendship. It beats saying nothing at all or telling someone to drop dead.

It serves as a sort of conversational lubricant. The more people we pack into our cities, the more isolated they feel. We just trudge through the day, avoiding any kind of verbal contact that seems to call for personal involvement. Wishing someone a nice day is a way of speaking to a stranger without making any kind of long-term commitment.

Maybe it would help if Mayor William H. McNichols Jr. proclaimed an annual "Have-a-Nice-Day Day." People could elevate their awareness about what it means to wish someone a nice day. It wouldn't be one of those throwaway lines. On that one day, at least, people would really mean it, or pretend they did.

I have given some thought to the doctor's view that the expression is trite. He seems to want conversations concluded with more substantive matter.

How about telling the waitress who brings you coffee and a Danish, "Thanks a lot, Joyce, and by the way, tension in the Middle East was heightened Sunday when Israeli warplanes destroyed a nuclear reactor in Iraq."

That's a little heavy-going for early morning casual talk. She might get to brooding and pour hot coffee into the next customer's lap. You certainly wouldn't want something like that on your conscience.

What we really need are conversational fillers. They could be something like the short paragraphs newspapers use to fill out space at the end of a column. They aren't used much anymore because computers now make fitting stories more exact.

Ben Blackburn, our managing editor, said his favorite filler was, "At birth, the kangaroo is about the size of a peanut and is semitransparent." That is a dandy, but it would be a little difficult to work it into a conversation with the Avon lady.

The same is true for "Allentown, Pa., had 125,672 telephones in 1975." Good, solid stuff, but it does seem a little out of place in everyday badinage.

Suppose you run into an old Dartmouth classmate you haven't seen in years. "Dink! Is that you? Good Lord, it has been years. Haven't seen old Dink since the '56 Winter Carnival."

You and old Dink spend a few minutes comparing hairlines, wives and golf handicaps. You glance at your watch and see you're running a bit late.

"Dink! Good old Dink! Can't tell you how good it's been. Best to Marge. Let's have lunch. Maybe tennis, what? Do make it soon, Dink. Really. Mustn't lose touch. And by the way, Dink, Gertrude Ederle was the first woman to swim the English Channel."

Say something like that and old Dink will go home and tell Marge your arteries have hardened. He probably would be even less interested to know that the breeding grounds of the whooping crane were finally discovered in 1952.

Another alternative is to commit to memory a number of inspirational quotations. "Hey, Wally. After bowling, let's get a six-pack and we'll go over to my place and catch Friday night baseball on the tube. And Wally, as Henry Wadsworth Longfellow put it, 'Look not mournfully to the past . . . it comes not back again; go forth to meet the shadowy future without fear, and with a manly heart.' "

Wally probably will proceed to meet the shadowy future, but it is going to be on someone else's bowling team, six-pack or no. Forget Friday night baseball.

Have a nice day.

June 9, 1981

Governor leaves no tern unstoned

MIXED.

"The metaphor is probably the most fertile power possessed by man," wrote Jose Ortega y Gasset. That being the case, Gov. Richard D. Lamm has become a veritable dynamo of energy. His legendary "I am going to drive a silver stake through the heart of I-470" proves that.

I have always liked Lamm's approach to language. At a press conference during his first term he exclaimed, "That would really be a plum in our cap!" The Rocky Mountain News account of the incident was illustrated by a caricature of Lamm wearing a cap covered with plums.

Our Joan Lowy recalls a campaign speech Lamm made in 1982 before employees of the Manville Corp. Someone asked him if he might run for the Senate in the future. Lamm tried to quote William Tecumseh Sherman's message to the Republican National Convention in 1884 in which he said, "I will not accept if nominated and will not serve if elected."

But out of Lamm's mouth came the words, "If nominated I will not serve and if elected I will not run."

And then there was his unforgettable "That's the bale of hay that broke the camel's back." We all remember his "coasting on our laurels." One of my favorites is "The buck is in their corner."

Now that he is in his twilight years as Colorado governor, it is refreshing to know that he has not lost his touch. In a lecture at the Pacific School of Religion last month, Lamm spoke to what he called "our shrinking agricultural base."

"While the demands on American generosity have been growing, our resources have been shrinking," Lamm said. "The stork is flying faster than the plow."

We all ran to the window, pointed to the sky and said in unison: "Is it a bird? Is it a plane? It's a plow!"

The stork-plow analogy was not something Lamm blurted out. It was part of a carefully written text. A race between the stork and the plow is more one-sided than the one between the tortoise and the hare.

It also conjures up images of a sky filled with plows, banking, turning, flying in formation and landing at Stapleton International Airport. "This is United Plow Lines Flight 365 making a final approach on runway three-five, over."

But maybe he was trying to misquote the Bible by saying, "They shall beat their plowshares into swords, and their pruninghooks into spears."

I suppose Lamm was making the point we are raising babies faster than we are raising corn. But that's not really colorful enough. Anyone who hopes to be quoted by others must be able to turn phrases that are catchy and create mental images.

While Lamm still commits an occasional mixed metaphor or malapropism, he does so less frequently than during his first term.

He may get over it entirely. He still has two years to go. And after all, as the old saying goes, "Rome wasn't burned in a day."

I am a fine one to talk. My command of language is not as firm as it might be. As another adage counsels us, "People who live in glass houses should gather no moss."

February 19, 1985

Lamm's tongue does have a point

GAFFE.

Our silver-tongued governor has done it again, hasn't he? Just as the furor was dying out over his candid observations about prostitutes in Las Vegas, Nev., Richard D. Lamm has now angered elderly Coloradans.

By suggesting that terminally ill old people have a "duty to die and get out of the way," Lamm has added yet another gem to what has become a legendary list of boo-boos dating from his first term in office. You'll recall it all began in 1976 when he commanded a room full of journalists to "stand up, dammit!"

Lamm got carried away when the Denver Broncos went to the Super Bowl in 1978 but was finally persuaded not to declare a state holiday in the team's honor. Then he drove a "silver stake" into the heart of the proposed I-470 highway project.

Characterizing himself as a modern "Paul Revere," our plucky governor says he is only trying to alert us to important social issues. But he also must understand it is somewhat jarring to be awakened in the night to a shout of "The undertaker is coming! The undertaker is coming!"

While Lamm may not be getting any more tactful as he gets older, his style has certainly become more poetic. He demonstrated this in a speech before the Colorado Health Lawyers Association when he compared senior citizens who die naturally to "leaves falling off a tree and forming humus for the other plants to grow up."

That's sort of the way I have looked at the life cycle, but then I'm not the governor. And I may change my tune when it is my leaf that begins to fall. I have known for some time, however, that while everyone wants to go to heaven, few of us want to die to get there.

Perhaps his original quote on the "duty to die" was paraphrased and taken out of context, but it does conjure a scene in which poor old Aunt Tillie looks up from her bed at Old Glory standing unfurled in the corner of her hospital room. She manages a brave little salute, and then she gamely reaches down and unplugs her life-support system.

All of the imagery of humus and falling leaves aside, Lamm is correct when he suggests we can no longer afford to pursue technological immortality for its own sake. It doesn't seem to me Lamm advocates euthanasia so much as he counsels us that artificial means of sustaining organic life long beyond consciousness do a disservice to those yet unborn. He also seems to be saying that the quality of life is at least as important as its length.

Often lost in Lamm's blunt way of speaking is the truth of his message. His controversial ideas on controlling health-care costs, urban growth and illegal immigration become easily sensationalized. But he is right more often than he is wrong.

And besides, from this perspective, I would rather have a governor who makes an occasional gaffe when he says what needs to be said, than one who bores us stiff and never says anything.

Quote: *If I could drop dead right now, I'd be the happiest man alive.* — Samuel Goldwyn.

April 1, 1984

A yuppie a day makes one weary

SNEAKERS.

The Idea Fairy was wearing her dressed-for-success suit when she came into the newsroom. Her shirt was a blue oxford cloth with button-down collar. Her tie was neatly knotted, and she was wearing tennis socks and Nike running shoes.

ME — Well, what do we have here? Don't we look upwardly mobile today.

FAIRY — I have my wing-tipped pumps in my attache case.

ME — Are you a yuppie?

FAIRY — Yes. I am very much into Chablis, Brie cheese, networking, taking care of my body and pinpointing my aggression level.

ME — Is all that involved in being a young urban professional?

FAIRY — And a lot more. I have a 10-speed bicycle, a personal computer and an American Express credit card. But what about you? You wear running shoes. Does that make you a yuppie?

ME — No. I am an ounpie.

FAIRY — An ounpie?

ME — Yes. That's an old urban non-professional.

FAIRY — Journalism isn't a profession?

ME — No. Medicine, law, teaching, accounting and prostitution are professions. Journalism is a craft, much like carpentry, plumbing, brick laying and basket weaving.

FAIRY — But running shoes? You don't run.

ME — I wear them because they are comfortable on my poor old arthritic feet. I don't care what they look like. If running shoes make me look like a yuppie, so be it. Thomas Hornsby Ferril wears sneakers. No one accuses him of being a yuppie.

FAIRY — Mr. Ferril, the poet laureate of Colorado, wears sneakers?

ME — You bet he does. He likes the old style high tops. The kind Dolly McGlone recommended when he was my gym teacher at Byers Junior High.

FAIRY — Does Mr. Ferril run?

ME — No, but he walks around Smith Lake at Washington Park every morning. He also likes the shoes because they are comfortable when he dances the bolero.

FAIRY — Ravel's "Bolero"?

ME — You bet. Tom can even play it on the mandolin. The only mandolin version ever done of "Bolero." As the insistent tempo builds and begins to throb, Tom gets very emotional. He can also play Beethoven's "Eroica" symphony and "Jesus Wants Me for a Sunbeam."

FAIRY — Why don't we have people like that anymore?

ME — We don't need them. We have Ferril.

FAIRY — Getting back to yuppies, do you approve of them?

ME — I like them better than the self-absorbed young people of the 1970s, but not as well as the rebellious kids of the '60s. Yuppies are better than the dull "Happy Days" bunch of the '50s, but they don't hold a candle to those magnificent, courageous, fun-filled, world beaters of the 1940s — the last of the great decades.

FAIRY — Hey, where are you going?

ME — Home to get out my Glenn Miller records.

January 13, 1985

2

TWILIGHT TIME

Don't knock the jock

STUPEFYING.

Ayatollah Ruhollah Khomeini has demanded that all music be banned from Iranian radio broadcasts. Not only does it stupefy, the bearded spiritual leader said, but it also takes people "out of reality to a futile and lowly livelihood."

For once, the old boy may be onto something. He won't get much argument from American disc jockeys. If anyone has come in contact with the evils of music, the nation's record spinners certainly have.

Spend all day, every day with phonograph records and you'll wind up on the funny farm. It doesn't matter what kind of music. The result is the same. Bubb-ah-dee-bubb-ah-dee-bubb.

Disc jockeys pretend they are having a good time and like the music they play. They do not. Once they start to play a record, they turn down the volume on the studio monitor so they can have a little blessed silence.

Their fraudulent enthusiasm can be excused only because there is little else in life they are qualified to do. Think of it as another way of dealing with the indigent.

Announcers on MOR (middle of road) radio stations have gray hair and pot bellies. DJs on jazz stations have congenital laryngitis.

People who work at "beautiful music" FM stations are the lucky ones. Their programming is automated and on tape and no one has to listen. It is the sort of music one hears in elevators.

The announcers on country and western stations are particularly unfortunate. The music they play is so depressing. It is about infidelity and the diesel fuel shortage. The DJ seeks solace by looking at pictures of Dolly Parton.

Progressive-rock disc jockeys have a certain vagueness about their delivery. This is because they are never quite sure whether the record is playing or not.

The people who spin platters on "teenie-rock" or "bubblegum" stations are not real. Legend has it that they are found under cabbage leaves.

The most wretched of all are those who broadcast over classical music stations. One old-timer, who declined use of his name, put it this way: "All those years of playing Boston Pops records have turned my mind to yogurt."

He had been a disc jockey on virtually every other kind of musical format before he did his classical gig. "I had to find someplace to spend my declining years," he said. "I thought there'd be some peace and quiet.

"But I was wrong. Same old rat race. It's even tougher because of the language. Experience has taught me never to play anything I can't pronounce. There is nothing a classical listener enjoys more than calling up and sticking it to the poor slob on the air because he mispronounced some obscure composer's name."

The old man's chin began to quiver as he talked. "It has been my private view for years that opera is nothing more than a bunch of fat people screaming at each other.

"Do you realize that most of the music we play around here was written by people who are no longer alive? I say, let them rest in peace."

Is there any fun left in it for him? The aging broadcaster managed a little smile and said, "Some. The other day I announced that Annette Funicello was one of the singers in the sextet from Lucia di Lammermoor. The idea of a mouseketeer in a bikini bathing suit, singing Donizetti, just wiped me out."

What does he fear the most? "Toppling over while a record of Ravel's 'Bolero' is playing. I can't stand that music. It is monotony on top of monotony. I just know, though, that when my time comes, it will be when that damned music is playing.

"I also have problems with organ music. It loosens the fillings in my teeth and aggravates my arthritis. After I play a record of one of those Bach fugues, I tremble for hours. What radio needs today is a little more quiet," he said.

Quote: *Organs are placed in churches as a means of punishing sinners.* — T. Milliken Gavin.

July 27, 1979

Announcer fades into the sunrise

PASSAGES.

My first day in broadcasting was spent in the KMYR studios, 1626 Stout St. My last day came Wednesday, just one-half block away and 42 years later on the 29th floor of the Petro Lewis Building, 17th and Stout streets.

Serious young men wearing dark suits and expensive shaving lotion shuffled through stacks of legal documents in the penthouse board room of the Hall and Evans law firm. I sat at one end of the long table with my lifetime friend and business partner, Ed Koepke. We were there to sign away our ownership of radio station KVOD.

As I wrote my name hundreds of times on papers I shall never read, it occurred to me that my broadcast career ended as it had begun — as an announcer. It is a classic example of the "Peter Principle." I had quickly risen to my level of incompetence and had remained there all those years. Once an announcer, always an announcer.

Ed, on the other hand, started as a studio engineer and made his way up through various levels of broadcast executive responsibility to the top. Regardless of what we actually did, we were 50-50 partners in all of the media enterprises we have owned over the years.

I have always regretted that so much of the credit came to me for what both of us have accomplished. I was always the one in the spotlight. Ed stayed in the background. We have never had a single argument. I suppose our skills complemented each other's. I once overheard someone say: "Koepke is the brains. Amole is the mouth."

There is no arguing the truth of that. In reflecting on the 26 years we have owned KVOD and its predecessors, Ed and I are gratified by the large number of people who have been exposed for the first time to classical music by listening to our station.

I think I know why classical music is becoming so popular among young people. It helps meet a need we all have for structure in our lives. The traditional institutions of home, government, church and school are no longer able to satisfy our personal needs for order. The structure of classical music helps fill the void.

If modern society is accurately mirrored by the anxiety of contemporary rock music, as I believe it is, then classical music tells us how an ideal society ought to be. It is a little easier to face the day when it begins with Mozart.

We have always believed classical music belongs to everyone. It is not just for the affluent, the well-educated, the socially elite. Our approach is to be ourselves on the air and not look down our noses if people mispronounce a composer's name, or don't know what a continuo is.

I have been frequently asked how I feel about leaving broadcasting. There is no way I can describe the conflicting emotions I had that last day. Ed and I will sorely miss the lovely people with whom we have worked these years. Our staff includes: Shirley Ahlstrom, Steve Blatt, Dick Brehm, Jennifer Hart, Lisa Hartman, Willa Hatcher, Ted Mann, Marie Rodgers, Charley and Jocko Samson, Betsy "Boo" Veto, Maggie Welch, Lynda Watkins, Jake Williams, John Wolfe and Terry McDonald and his dog, Little Spike.

I shall particularly miss listeners to "Music for a New Day." There is a strong bond between us. We have shared sunrises, waltzes, bird songs, marches, tangos, a few laughs, hymns and so much more. I will have to live with the emptiness of losing many radio friends, most of whom I have never seen. That is the tough part.

The bright side of my departure from KVOD is Lisa Hartman. I selected her as my replacement a year ago. She is doing an excellent job and will be even better, now that I'm not looking over her shoulder all the time.

Lisa is talented, bright, enthusiastic, eager to work hard and not temperamental. And, hey, she does excellent commercials, so important in today's brutally competitive broadcast marketplace. As I have often said, classical music may be divinely inspired, but God doesn't sign pay checks. KVOD gets no foundation or government grants. It struggles for the buck as do all commercial stations.

Ed and I are delighted Charlton Buckley has purchased KVOD. He has made a commitment to continue classical music broadcasting in Denver. I have thought for some time KVOD needs new blood, new leadership, perhaps some new directions. Buckley is fortunate to have an outstanding staff upon which he can rely to improve the product.

I had thought I would quietly tip-toe out the back door when the end of my broadcast career came. But it was not to be. I am a little embarrassed at all the news media attention it has attracted. I suspect there must be a hard-news shortage.

As KVOD seeks new directions, so will Ed and I. Our partnership will endure and will be known as K&A Enterprises. Of course I shall continue with my column at the Rocky Mountain News. I have great affection for this old newspaper. I want to get better at what I do here, and Lord knows, there is plenty of room for improvement.

Quote: *The happy highways where I went and cannot come again.* — A.E. Housman.

December 11, 1983

'M' is for Mozart, music and magic

ALONE.

Only a gravedigger was present when Wolfgang Amadeus Mozart was buried in Vienna Dec. 6, 1791. He had died of heart failure a day earlier, convinced he had been poisoned by his archrival, Antonio Salieri.

But it was rheumatic fever, an ailment plaguing him since childhood. Mozart was 35 when he died, but is remembered today as the greatest musical genius of all time.

Thursday is the 227th anniversary of his birth. And if Salieri were alive, he would still be lamenting his misfortune at not having Mozart's talent. In the hit Broadway play "Amadeus," the pious Salieri can't understand why God didn't choose him through which to channel such magnificent music instead of the disreputable Mozart.

And magnificent it is. In the parlance of today's TV sportscasters, "Mozart could do it all," or "he had all the tools." His 700 or so compositions are in 23 categories. "Don Giovanni" is believed by many to be the greatest opera ever written.

Not all his writings were sublime. Mozart's letters to a cousin, Maria Anna Thekla, were disgustingly vulgar. He was constantly in debt.

Mozart's music has special appeal to children, perhaps because he began composing minuets when he was only 5. His "Ah Vous Dirai Je Mamman" variations, K. 265, are really a piano exploration of "Twinkle, Twinkle, Little Star." He was composing symphonies at age 10 when the rest of us were out playing Little League baseball.

Robert Horskey, an instructor at Denver's Goldrick Elementary School, teaches Mozart's music to his fourth-, fifth-, and sixth-graders. Parents who worry that their children are exposed only to punk rock should read fan mail that Horskey's kids have written to Mozart on his birthday.

Lisa Turja wrote: *Dear Mr. Mozart: I like your groovy music. You must have been smart when you were little.*

Angela Darlington seemed influenced by Frank Zappa's "Valley Girls" in her letter: *To Wolfgang: Your music is TOTALLY the best. Your orchestra music is out of this WORLD.*

Tim Mondragon composed some doggerel: *You are dead and gone/but your music still plays on. You were once on this earth./227 years ago was your birth.*

Kristine Friesen also made up a rhyme: *Mozart, you are number one/And your music is very well done. If you were alive today/you would be great in every way.*

Sandy Patricia Fagrelius took a different approach: *Dear Wolfgang: Your music is exciting. It makes my heart beat fast. Your music will always be at the top of the charts for me. Your music is as smooth as fur.*

Janel Castro put it right on the line: *You must have had magic to write the music you wrote. Your music is the greatest and I want you to know that.*

Thuy Lee's letter provided some nice imagery: *Wolfgang — a genius musician. You ought to be king. Your music is like a rainbow reaching out to touch the world.*

Mozart may have died alone, but he is in excellent company today.

January 27, 1983

Language of music is changed forever

TRUTH.

Thursday, March 21, 1985, isn't just another day at the office. It is a day to celebrate the 300th anniversary of the birth of Johann Sebastian Bach and a time to consider the importance of structure in our lives.

For me, it is difficult to write about Bach's music. Just as good poetry makes its own statement, Bach's music is its own eloquence. Explanations are superfluous. The problem is to convince people they don't need to be musical eggheads to find pleasure and meaning in Bach's music.

Albert Schweitzer believed that all musical roads lead to Bach and that none goes beyond. Other Bach students are not that dogmatic. One thing is clear: He was an unbiased seeker of truth. At his death in 1750, the language of music was changed forever. Bach said the last word on every musical form he touched. He had no imitators.

Musical scholars love to pounce on Bach's occasional lapses. A seemingly pointless aria becomes a "gotcha!" And the critics chew endlessly on the "pictorialism" in his music. Pictorialism is when a composer writes a score to match the words. The practice began in the late Renaissance when Claudio Monteverdi declared language the master of music, not the other way around as had been the tradition in the composition of music for madrigals.

Bach was his own severest critic. As in his "Passion According to St. John," he frequently revised and shortened his works, often discarding superb arias or chorales, but crafting a shorter work that was perfect.

But what does all that mean to us today? In a chaotic contemporary world, what is the value of centuries-old cantatas, concertos, suites, fugues and chorales? Why does Bach loom as such an imposing and dominating figure in the arts?

There is no single answer for all. But for me, the music of Bach meets a need for structure in my life. When institutions of home, church and state seem near collapse, I draw great strength and reassurance simply by listening to the sublime chorale prelude to Bach's Cantata No. 140, *Wachet auf, ruft uns die Stimme* (Awake, the voice cries to us). Indeed it does!

Because of this music's simple beauty and unassailable logic, I am able to use it as a bedrock foundation upon which to rebuild the architecture of my belief in life and humankind. For me, this is one of the great gifts of classical music.

If, for example, punk music mirrors contempt for our disoriented world, then the music of Bach tells us how our world ought to be. We all have an emotional requirement for that kind of order and structure. Bach's music responds to that need.

The Concerto in D minor for two violins B.W.V. 1043 is my favorite Bach composition. It has tension in its opening *vivace* movement, release in its lyrical *largo ma non tanto* and a most satisfying resolution in the concluding *allegro* movement.

There is great pleasure awaiting those for whom March 21 is "just another day at the office." Ready for their discovery is the priceless beauty, structure and truth in the music of Johann Sebastian Bach.

March 21, 1985

The value of versatility

EXPERIENCE.

The Idea Fairy was sitting on the edge of my new telephone directory when I walked up to my desk in the newsroom. She had one of those "No. 1" badges pinned to the lapel of her tiny khaki blazer.

ME — Where did you get your badge?

FAIRY — Ralph Looney gave it to me. He said he was very proud of all of us for making the Rocky Mountain News the biggest newspaper in Colorado.

ME — The new circulation figures?

FAIRY — Yes. The ones showing us ahead of The Denver Post on Sundays as well as on weekdays.

ME — Did you get a piece of the cake they brought into the newsroom?

FAIRY — I just pretended to eat it. I'm trying to get back into my party dress before the holidays. By the way, who was that young man who was interviewing you over in the corner?

ME — His name is Robert Lee. He's learning broadcasting at the Career Education Center. That's the wonderful school near North High where kids from all Denver high schools study for specific careers.

FAIRY — He's going into media work?

ME — Yes. He asked how I got into this business and where I get my ideas.

FAIRY — You told him about me?

ME — Certainly.

FAIRY — Anything else?

ME — I stressed the importance of writing short sentences. I also advised him to write to express, not to impress.

FAIRY — It's tough for kids to break into this game. Did anyone ever help you?

ME — No. I just kept pounding on doors until one of them opened. I was lucky my first job was in a small radio station. That way I had to learn to do many things.

FAIRY — Jack of all trades?

ME — I suppose. But so many young people these days are

training to be specialists. They know how to do just one thing. When they burn out on that, they have no backup skills.

FAIRY — Who is the best all-around broadcaster in Denver?

ME — That's what Peter Boyles asked me the other morning on his KOA talk show. I told him Bob Martin is the most versatile radio man I know. Most everyone thinks he just knows sports. Bob can do it all. If you ask him, he will tell you much of his success resulted from starting in a small radio station in Illinois.

FAIRY — Have you been taking Horatio Alger pills lately?

ME — No. It's just that kids want to start at the top. They don't understand that half the fun is making the climb. Getting there has its rewards, but the real excitement is in the struggle.

FAIRY — You're not thinking of retiring altogether, are you?

ME — No. I am still learning short, declarative sentence structure. There is much more for me to study.

FAIRY — Why haven't you ever learned to use the colon in your writing?

ME — My education was spotty: It lacked both continuity and structure.

FAIRY — Oh.

November 6, 1983

Gershwins give us a sense of direction

'S WONDERFUL.

A musical era didn't end with the death of Ira Gershwin. So long as there is an America, we'll have the music of George and Ira Gershwin to remind us who we are, where we came from and where we want to go.

The Gershwins probably didn't appreciate the enduring quality of their own creativity. They saw their music as firmly grounded in time. Their America came into flower at the end World War I, and they captured the tempo of their times.

They began in 1918 with their "The Real American Folk Song is a Rag." Their last song before George's death in 1937 was "Love is Here to Stay." It was an appropriate coda of their collaboration. Their 32-bar music, like love, is certainly here to stay. As their song put it, "They Can't Take That Away From Me."

Weren't their songs about the Depression, prosperity, dark clouds with silver linings and all the other symbols of the '20s and '30s? Sure. But the music was not really that trendy. It remains a lyrical foundation for our American Dream.

I don't know that Ira Gershwin ever knew of Claudio Monteverdi, the 16th century composer. They had a great deal in common, however. Monteverdi was the first to accept a proposition that lyrics should dominate music. And because of that belief, he invented opera as we know it today.

Take, for example, what many consider *the* American opera, "Porgy and Bess." The music George wrote for "It Ain't Necessarily So" is every bit as skeptical as Ira's lyrics. Listen to the melody in your mind as Sportin' Life sings: *Me-thus'-lah lived nine hundred years,/But who calls dat liv-in'/When no gal 'll give in/To no man what's nine hundred years?*

The opera may have been composed in 1935, but the truth of life along Catfish Row is eternal. When the Gershwins wrote their political satire, "Strike Up the Band," in 1927, they weren't just exposing the body politic of the Roaring Twenties, they were doing it for all time. There is a Sen. Throttlebottom in every session of Congress.

Like George, Ira had style. He was witty and literate. But the two were as different as brothers could be. The sometimes frenetic George loved the spotlight. Ira was shy, unhurried, calm.

As with most creative people, he was constantly questioning his own ability. Almost daily he faced the agony all writers know of finding new ways to utter old truths. He was never satisfied with his "Love Walked In" because "it doesn't say anything new." It escaped him that the song said something everlasting.

That Ira could write for composers other than his brother said much of his mastery of the craft. He was equally successful in his collaborations with Irving Caesar, B.G. De Sylva, Ballard Macdonald, Vernon Duke, Harold Arlen, Harry Warren, Jerome Kern, Kurt Weill and Aaron Copland.

The music of these composers, as well as of his brother's, is firmly, permanently and happily anchored to Ira Gershwin's words. What greater tribute is there for a lyricist? His music:

" 'S mar-ve-lous!"

August 21, 1983

It's twilight time

PURPLE DUSK.

"Stardust" is really two songs. The verse and the chorus are so different they are frequently performed separately. Frank Sinatra and Tony Bennett often sing them that way.

The chorus is the more popular of the two. It's the part that begins: *Sometimes I wonder why I spend the lonely night/Dreaming of a song/The melody haunts my reverie,/And I am once again with you,/When our love was new, and each kiss an inspiration,/But that was long ago: now my consolation is the stardust of a song.*

Howard Hoagland "Hoagy" Carmichael composed the music. Hardly anyone remembers it was Mitchell Parrish who wrote the words. It is usually that way with popular music. Songs are remembered for their melodies.

In some ways, the verse of "Stardust" is lovelier than the chorus. Remember the lyrics? *And now the purple dusk of twilight time/ Steals across the meadows of my heart,/High up in the sky the little stars climb,/Always reminding me that we're apart.*

The first copyright on "Stardust" was by Mills Brothers Music Inc. in 1929. It was renewed by Belwin/Mills Publishing Corp. in 1957. Its real popularity, though, was in the late 1930s and early 1940s, when uncounted millions of couples claimed it as "our song."

I suppose a small part of them died when they learned Hoagy Carmichael had passed away at the age of 82. Rarely in the history of American music has a song enjoyed such universal popularity. "Stardust" became synonymous with the term "standard" in popular music. No band or combo would dare play in a public place without an arrangement of "Stardust" in its book. On the radio, it was perhaps the most requested song of all time.

"But that was long ago," as the lyric goes, and there are a couple of generations of Americans who have never heard of the song or its composer. Tenderness has all but disappeared from pop music.

Rock music is certainly reflective of the way society is today. It is filled with stress, anxiety and aggression. In Hoagy's time, music was more the way people wanted life to be. There was a great hunger for romance.

Not all of Hoagy's music was memorable. He turned out such turkeys as "Winter Moon," "Serenade to Gabriel," "Who Killed 'er (Who Killed the Black Widder)," "Hawaii, Pearls of the Sea," "Watermelon Weather," and the forgettable "My Christmas Song to You."

But we won't remember him that way. It will be "The Nearness of You," "Lazy Bones," "Two Sleepy People," "Ole Buttermilk Sky," "Small Fry," "Up the Lazy River," "Georgia on My Mind," "I Get Along Without You Very Well," and the 1951 Academy Award-winning "In the Cool of the Evening" that we'll associate with our memories of Hoagy. My favorites are "Skylark" and the sultry "Baltimore Oriole."

Those decades of the 1930s and the 1940s were not exclusively Hoagy Carmichael's, but he was certainly a part of their sound. Close your eyes and try to remember how it was.

The lights at the ballroom are low. The voice is Glenn Miller's: "And now, our Miller Medley. Something old, something new, something borrowed, something blue. Our old song tonight is Hoagy Carmichael's immortal 'Stardust.'"

And then we would hold each other and slowly dance to "The memory of love's refrain." Let me tell you something, those were very special times. Hoagy is gone, but we still have his music.

Quote: *You wandered down the lane and far away./Leaving me a song that will not die.* — from the lyric to "Stardust" by Mitchell Parrish.

December 31, 1981

Cole Porter's de-lovely lyrics

NIGHT AND DAY YOU ARE THE ONE,/ONLY YOU BENEATH THE MOON AND under the sun,/Whether near to me or far/It's no matter, darling, where you are,/I think of you, night and day./Day and night, why is it so/That this longing for you follows wherever I go?/In the roaring traffic's boom,/In the silence of my lonely room,/I think of you, night and day.

If you are thinking they don't write songs like that anymore, it's because composer-lyricist Cole Porter died in 1964. Had he lived, he would have observed his 93rd birthday Saturday. (Or 91st or 92nd, depending on the source.)

So much of today's rock music is devoid of love. It is hostile, angry, surly. Its sex-without-love theme is illustrated by one song in which a male narrates, but does not sing, "Hey, I don't sleep with your friends, and you don't sleep with mine."

Porter thought love and sex ought to be fun. Mary Martin launched her Broadway career in 1938 with a partial striptease while singing, *While tearing off/A game of golf/I may make a play for the caddy./But when I do/I don't follow through/'Cause my heart belongs to Daddy.*

Scholars of American mores and folkways over the past 60 years would do well to examine closely the lyrics of the more than 800 Cole Porter songs. He brought to the songwriting craft what John Updike described as "a great verbal ingenuity, a brave flexibility." Example: *So sweet to waken with,/So nice to sit down to eggs and bacon with.* ("Easy to Love").

Born in Peru, Ind., Porter attended Yale and Harvard, joined the French Foreign Legion and became a member of the lost generation of literary exiles in Europe. He returned home to mock propriety, to celebrate ambiguity and to become the nation's prince of urbane cheer.

As one who chronicled change, Porter had no peer. Close your eyes and listen to Ethel Merman sing: *In olden days, a glimpse of stocking/Was looked on as something shocking,/But now, God knows,/Anything goes./Good authors too who once knew better words/Now only use four-letter words/Writing prose,/Anything goes.*

But when Porter wrote lyrics, not everything did go. He discarded these: *In her garden, Mother Eve/Wore a fig leaf, we believe,/But this was no success/She went out and bought a dress,/Then the weather turning cold,/Mother Eve, so we are told,/To resist the wintry air/Bought herself some underwear./From then on, the gals their pretty bodies bolstered/Till a lady wasn't dressed, she was upholstered.*

He knew these lyrics were right: *It's the wrong time and the wrong place,/Though your face is charming, it's the wrong face,/It's not her face but such a charming face/That it's all right with me . . .*

What's left to say of Cole Porter's music? *It's delightful, it's delicious,/It's delectable, it's delirious,/It's dilemma, it's delimit, it's deluxe,/It's de-lovely.*

(Material from "The Complete Lyrics of Cole Porter," edited by Robert Kimball.)

June 10, 1984

'The Count' left mark on 'Studio A'

TASTE.

The program ended at 5 p.m. I had scooped up my commercials and records and was getting ready to leave when "The Kid from Red Bank" asked if he might play the studio Hammond organ for a few minutes.

It was 1946. William "Count" Basie was playing a one-nighter at O.K. Farr's Rainbow Ballroom. He was in the old KMYR "Studio A" to be interviewed on "Meet the Boys in the Band," a record show I was doing at the time.

Those "few minutes" lengthened into more than three hours. I sat alone in the studio and listened to Count Basie play an unforgettable concert for an audience of one. As I listened, I pretended it was all for me, but I knew all along it was really Basie playing for Basie.

That was the first of many times I had the pleasure of interviewing Bill Basie, as most of his friends called him. He was one of the most polite, gentle, generous and accommodating public figures I have ever known.

His love for the organ went back to 1922 when he studied piano informally in Harlem with the great Fats Waller, also a devotee of the organ. It was during that same period Basie met and was influenced by James P. Johnson.

Basie played "stride" piano then, as did most of his contemporaries. It wasn't until the mid-1930s in Kansas City that he changed his technique to that economical, bluesy sound he employed until his death. He used tasty melodic right-hand leads and cues to maintain rhythmic control of the powerful band behind him. No one ever successfully imitated that style.

Even though he was born in Red Bank, N.J., Basie's name became synonymous with the Kansas City tradition of organizing the big band around a rhythm section as Benny Moten and Jay McShann had done.

And what a rhythm section! Basie was on piano, of course; Walter Page, bass; Jo Jones, drums; Freddie Green, guitar. The section's distinctive sound was caused in no small part by Jones' use of the high-hat, rather than the bass drum, to drive the tempo. No one, before or since, could play the high-hat like Jo Jones.

This supple but solid rhythm section provided soloists superb backing. Similarly, the brass and reeds could explore endless riff possibilities as in "Jumpin' at the Woodside," "One O'Clock Jump," "Music Makers" and the early "Song of the Islands."

There is no space here to list all the soloists whose roots are deeply imbedded in the Basie tradition. But certainly tenor saxophonist Lester "Prez" (for president) Young deserves special mention. His cool, highly personal style not only inspired the band but strongly influenced future generations of saxophonists. There were many ot~ers: Buck Clayton, Harry "Sweets" Edison, "Little" Jimmy Rushing, Helen Humes, Dickie Wells, Don Bayas, Joe Williams.

Bill Basie was an American original, a man of exquisite musical taste. He will not be replaced.

Ever.

April 29, 1984

3

HERE'S LOOKING AT YOU

A letter to Mikey, beyond the hurt

DEAR MIKEY:

Knowing you have been out of touch, I thought I would drop you a line to bring you up to date on what has happened since Dec. 17, 1982, the day you were beaten to death. It is such a sad story.

Too bad you missed Christmas. There was lots of snow. The foothills near Boulder were very white and beautiful. Santa brought presents and candy to your little friends in the housing project.

You were missed almost immediately. When Mommy wouldn't tell police where you were, she was arrested Dec. 30. She said she was afraid if she told officers where you were, you would be taken away from her. That was really kind of silly since Mommy later told police she had kept your dead body in the apartment for a week before she and Danny buried you.

Not much happened for the next three months. It was just a lot of boring police and lawyer stuff. Finally, after 102 days of silence, Mommy broke down and admitted to the officers that you were dead, and she told them where you were buried.

Danny was arrested April 11. The officers started looking for your body that afternoon. They dug most of the night and next morning. When they found you in that northeast Boulder irrigation ditch, you were wrapped in a green blanket inside an old vinyl shower curtain. It was very sad for those policemen when they took you out of the ground. We had all hoped you were still alive somewhere.

You were given a more proper burial April 18 in the baby-land section of Boulder's Mountain View Memorial Park. The coffin was white and there was a wreath of white carnations on top. There were 300 people, including your sister, Tricia, your aunt Cecilia and your grandma. The day was filled with sunshine.

Both Mommy and Danny were charged with your murder. Danny's trial is winding down now. It was sort of like a game, with one bunch of lawyers trying to beat the other. The defense lawyers won, getting Danny's charges reduced from first-degree murder to felony child abuse.

Mommy's trial will be next. It isn't likely she will be convicted, what with all the legal rigmarole. Some say Mommy beat you to death. Others say Danny did it. Someone certainly did. Only you know, and your tiny voice can't be heard now. Maybe they took turns beating you.

I wish I could explain to you why people are able to get away with beating and killing little kids like you. The grown-ups have somehow made it possible for both truth and justice to fall through the cracks.

Mikey, I know that doesn't concern you now. You are beyond the beatings, the screaming, the torture and all the brutality that dominated your short, unhappy life. For you, the hurting has stopped. We can all be grateful for that.

I just wish you could have shared in the justice system that has been so generous to those who battered away your precious life. But it isn't to be. We are all so sorry we let you down.

Sincerely,
Geno

October 27, 1983

Children's trust perverted by lust

PEDOPHILIA.

"No! No!" the terrified child in the supermarket shouts. Running to his mother, he sobs that someone tried to touch him. An embarrassed man protests that he meant no harm. The mother demands to see the manager.

I think about a situation like that each time I see an appealing child in a public place. It used to be I thought nothing of approaching a small boy or girl and trying to make friends. I might have even patted the youngster on the head or bottom.

Not anymore. I think twice before I even smile or try to talk to children now that public awareness of child molestation is very high. That's one of the sad consequences of educational programs now being given small children.

Pedophilia is a clinical term for a sexual perversion in which children are preferred as sex objects. Its practitioners, pedophiles, are not always dirty old men with wrinkled raincoats and bags of candy.

"A pedophile is typically a male individual ... (who) knows his victim, is not dirty or old and looks and dresses like everyone else," according to FBI agent Kenneth Lanning, who testified last week before a Senate Judiciary subcommittee in Washington.

The subcommittee is looking into possible legislation requiring government agencies dealing with children to conduct background checks for criminal records on all potential employees.

Another FBI agent, Melvin Mercer Jr. of the identification division, told the subcommittee that it is difficult to distinguish between the "well-meaning nice people who like kids, and the perverted minority." While Mercer supports the spirit of the proposed legislation, he called instead for education programs to teach children that they have "the right to say no."

The difficulty of establishing a profile for child molesters is borne out by that case in California in which several staff members of a formerly respected child care center, including women, have been charged with sexually abusing children. None had any previous record of child abuse.

We really don't know whether the wave of reported cases of molestation indicates an increase in this kind of perversion or whether we are just letting the problem out of the closet.

Parents hope special education programs that teach toddlers to "say no" will afford them some protection from the "nice" man in the neighborhood who takes advantage of their trust in him.

I know all this is necessary. Children are vulnerable to molesters. But I hope a way can be found to make them cautious without destroying their natural trust in older people who aren't pedophiles and who simply enjoy the company of children.

Children and older people need each other. We can't permit panic to destroy the healthy relationships mutually beneficial to small children and older adults.

There are "nice" old men who are really nice. There is a special understanding between the young and the old. We must find a way to make our children careful but not fearful of people simply because they are older and are friendly.

April 17, 1984

Here's looking at you

THERE'S A CRUMB ON YOUR LIP.

One of life's worst moments is caused by a crumb on the lip. It can be the most major of distractions. Its presence has the power to plunge the human spirit into hopeless quandary. A tiny crumb on the lip has been known to chill the warmest of relationships.

Let us set the stage.

You and your friend are meeting for lunch. It might be a member of the Teamsters Union, a Roman Catholic nun, a resident of Cherry Hills Village, a used-car salesman, a stunning Vogue model, even a district judge. The crumb-on-the-lip affliction can strike anyone.

So there you are at the restaurant. You greet each other warmly. The two of you are seated at a nice table and you immediately order lunch.

The waiter brings a basket of hard rolls.

That's the beginning of it. You are really in for it now. The problem is hidden away in that basket. The rolls are fresh-baked. Crusts are crispy and the centers are soft and moist.

Delicious rolls.

Without even a pause in the conversation, your friend selects a roll, breaks it in half and butters it. Then comes the first bite. It always seems to happen on the first bite.

A crumb on the lip.

It can be the upper lip. Sometimes it happens to the lower. Or the corner of the mouth. But the crumb is there. It is there to stay. Somehow you know that.

Over the next hour, that tenacious little crumb will defy the law of gravity. It will successfully resist any attempt to dislodge it. The bond that holds it to the lip is firm, not to be broken.

Your first instinct is to simply say, "There's a crumb on your lip." But you won't do that. You don't want to embarrass your friend. And besides, it is your optimistic belief that the crumb will soon fall of its own accord.

No way.

It hangs in there. Even during animated conversation and frequent bursts of laughter, that stubborn little crumb manages to hold to its precarious position.

You try to avoid looking at the crumb. You stare intently at your cup of soup. The carnations in the bud vase. Your fingernails. Anything. But it doesn't work. Your eyes are drawn to that crumb as magnetically as the moth is to the flame.

Your next ploy is to invoke the power of suggestion. You frequently wipe your own mouth with your napkin. It is your desperate hope that your friend will take the hint. Also, you have a gnawing fear that there is one of those hated crumbs on your lip.

Even if your friend wipes frequently at the mouth with a napkin, that pesky crumb stays put. Sometimes it seems to flutter as it bobs up and down. It teeters. It swings. It dangles. But it doesn't fall off.

Not that crumb.

You will next be possessed by an almost uncontrollable urge. You will want to reach across the table and flick away that crumb with your hand. You will actually twitch in anticipation.

Try to avoid it. Excuse yourself and walk directly to the restroom. Compose yourself. Examine your face in the mirror for crumbs. Close your eyes tightly and say to yourself, "When I get back to the table, the crumb will be gone."

It won't.

It will be there and will remain on your friend's lip until the two of you part. You will note compassion in the eyes of others in the restaurant.

Your agony ends when the two of you go separate ways. You will always wonder where and when the crumb finally fell away. Your friend will be puzzled by your behavior at lunch. Apprehensive. Preoccupied.

Next time, stop it before it starts. After that first bite, look your friend in the eye and say, "There's a crumb on your lip."

August 21, 1978

No more waiting

STEAMED.

The longer I sat alone in that little room at the doctor's office, the more my blood pressure went up. Actually, it wasn't my blood pressure that brought me there. It was my stopped-up ear.

I have nerve deafness. Too many wars. Too many loud phonograph recordings in too many radio studios. It is one of those hearing loss problems for which there is no cure. A hearing aid doesn't help. It just makes the ringing louder.

When my case was first diagnosed, the doctor told me to learn to read lips. I haven't come to that yet. I'm OK in one-on-one conversation. The phone is no problem. It's the crowded room that gives me trouble.

Cocktail parties are the worst. Words jam together in a formless gibberish. I have learned to smile, nod and utter a little gibberish of my own. As I recall, cocktail party conversation is little more than gibberish anyhow.

My left ear became completely blocked with wax last week. I couldn't hear anything with it, not even gibberish. That's when I made an appointment with my ear doctor.

I had been going to this physician for maybe six or seven years. He is a nice man and a talented doctor. But when I arrived for my appointment, the receptionist acted as though I had never been there before.

She made me fill out new forms about insurance, whom to notify in case of an emergency, where I work, a list of my dependents — all that jazz. I tried to tell her she had the information, but she said there was no record of me.

A triage nurse then filled out more forms about the wax in my ear. Then she put me in a little room. That's where my blood pressure went up. There was one stool, one examination bench and one stainless steel cart with little hoses coming out of it.

Forty minutes passed and no one looked at the wax in my ear. I was left to read the instructions on the stainless steel cart and to look at before-and-after photographs of nose jobs the doctor had done.

I got up and walked out. A nurse followed me down the hall, telling me it wouldn't be much longer. I quietly told her that 40 minutes was too long to wait. I knew I had to get out of there before my blood pressure went crazy. I had started to remember all the wasted hours I had spent in doctors' offices over the years, and I really got steamed.

This is not a blanket indictment of all physicians. My regular doctor is very punctual. So is my dentist. But there are some doctors who take the attitude that there is nothing wrong with requiring a patient to spend a half-day just to get 10 minutes of treatment. I am not going to put up with that anymore.

The deadline at this newspaper is 7:15 p.m. If my column isn't ready by then, I get fired. The Federal Communications Commission will take away my radio station if I am repeatedly careless about timing. I have had to accommodate myself to those realities.

I understand that physicians, particularly surgeons and obstetricians, can't always maintain precise schedules. I am willing to give a little leeway. But I'll never again wait longer than 20 minutes for any medical service. Life is too short to spend it reading old magazines.

The bright side to this is that I found a quick, easy and inexpensive solution to my ear wax problem. By the next day, Sunday, I was in real agony. I went to that little walk-in medical emergency clinic at South Wadsworth Boulevard and West Hampden Avenue.

There was a minimum of paper work. A medical doctor and three nurses took care of my problem in a matter of minutes. The whole thing cost 26 bucks. They even filled out my insurance forms for me. There was a little sign on the desk that said I was welcome.

I appreciated that.

July 30, 1981

Flowers to mitigate hard-line rhetoric

Lilacs.

Someone must have forgotten to close my window of vulnerability. Spring finally slipped in. The air is sweet, the skies are filled with sunshine, blue jays are squabbling in the treetops. It is great to be alive.

I had thought winter was going to run right up to summer, but we are having spring after all. It is about one week behind schedule. Trees here are usually in full leaf the last week of May. My old cottonwood still has a way to go.

The late frost wasn't sufficiently sharp to more than just nip apple and cherry blossoms. Bright yellow forsythia survived, as did the lilacs. Frost killed most lilacs last year.

They are glorious this spring. A slight breeze summons their fragrance along the parkways. Blossoms are so heavy they bend branches to the ground.

Did you know the Russians have lilacs? It is the sort of thing one doesn't think about much. Russia has snow. Russia has onion-shaped domes on their buildings. Russia has uncounted divisions of identical soldiers. Russia has missiles. But lilacs?

Yes, I wouldn't have known about Russian lilacs either, had it not been for Russian composer Sergei Rachmaninoff, a dour man. Rachmaninoff was once described by fellow composer Igor Stravinsky as having "a 6½-foot scowl."

Even with his somberness, the old boy had a gentle side, evidenced by his lovely song, "Siryen," Op. 21, No. 5. He must have liked the melody, because in addition to the vocal version, he wrote his own piano transcription, playing it frequently in recital.

Siryen is Russian for lilacs. "The melody," a critic observed, "hovers principally within a limited tessitura, floating over an undulating and atmospheric accompaniment."

I am glad I didn't say that. My late father gave me good advice years ago about communicating ideas when he told me, "Don't try to put the silk pants on people."

I do like the idea that Russians and Americans have lilacs in common, if little else. If you are thinking lilacs are too fragile upon which to build a relationship, you may be right. Even so, I like it better than our continuing dependence upon escalation of nuclear weaponry to keep the peace.

That occurred to me when it was revealed last week that high-level Soviet and American representatives have been holding informal arms limitation talks in Denver. There have been two such gatherings in local hotels, according to Gen. Brent Scowcroft, chairman of President Reagan's strategic missile commission.

If there is to be a third, I hope it is soon. Instead of conferring in a hotel, they should go to Washington Park, spread out a blanket, and then talk it out beside a lilac bush.

Maybe the setting would serve to mitigate hard-line rhetoric and bellicosity. Perhaps those delicate blossoms might even be more than symbolic of our commonality.

The lilacs are a gentle reminder of how fragile and how temporary our life is on this planet, and how both sides must have a reverence for it if we are to survive.

Quote: *Never does nature say one thing and wisdom another.* — Juvenal.

May 29, 1983

Reader's block

PLAIN BROWN WRAPPER.

The March issue of National Geographic magazine came last week. I still haven't opened it. Hope to get around to it before next week.

That's the way it always has been with me and the National Geographic. My intentions are the best. It is the follow-through that comes up wanting.

There always seems to be something else to do. You know, go out in the kitchen and make a baloney sandwich. Watch TV. Take a nap.

The problem with not reading National Geographic is that you feel guilty. It is so wholesome and they've worked so hard to put it together. You sort of owe it to them to take off the wrapper and read about forbidden Tibet.

In my case, the guilt goes back to the very beginning. It must be at least 20 years since I received my embossed invitation to become a member of the National Geographic Society.

I can't remember exactly how the language went, but the invitation said the board of trustees had met and had approved my name for membership in the society. It was signed by both the president and the chairman of the board.

There was no advance indication that I was even being considered for this high honor. It was as flattering as being a college freshman and being rushed by Beta Theta Pi.

Anyhow, I sent in the money right away. I certainly didn't want to offend the trustees by not acting promptly. And besides, my support was urgently needed so that the society's research and exploration projects could continue full tilt.

I actually made a stab at reading the first few issues that came, plodding through the articles on entomology, arctic tundra and the like. It wasn't long before I reached the point where I just flipped through the pages, occasionally looking at some of the pictures.

Even though there were some months when no one in our family would open the magazine at all, we always tried to keep the current issue on the coffee table in the living room. It was our way of telling the world that we did more than watch Archie Bunker on television.

No one ever throws away back issues of National Geographic. They are stacked away in basements and garages. There is a vague notion they eventually will be read by someone. They may be put to use as research material for a high school term paper.

The only people who have found a use for old issues of National Geographic are dentists. They place them in their waiting rooms as a means of punishing patients who neglect their teeth.

There is no better way of terrorizing and intimidating a patient than forcing him to listen to "Sioux City Sue" on the background music system while reading an article on Nepal from a 1946 issue of National Geographic.

It is the dentist's way of telling you how lax you have been with your home periodontal care. These lapses must be punished by bleeding gums and by reading old issues of National Geographic.

There are people out there who actually read every issue of National Geographic. I don't know who they are. I suspect, however, that the men have leather elbow patches on their tweed jackets and the women wear Enna Jetticks shoes.

My membership in the society is about up for renewal. There will be a reminder in the mail from the president, the chairman and the trustees.

I suppose I'll sign up again. Wouldn't want to hurt their feelings. Maybe there is a way out. I could return the letter unopened with a single word across the front of the envelope.

Deceased.

February 26, 1980

Ode to the geezer, a real big pleaser

AFFECTION.

The Idea Fairy was blotting her lipstick on a tiny Kleenex tissue when I came into the newsroom.

FAIRY — Got your valentines mailed yet?

ME — I have never been big on Valentine's Day.

FAIRY — You don't believe in romance?

ME — Sure. It's just that I have problems expressing affection. And Valentine's Day is too organized. Everyone is supposed to feel romantic all at the same time.

FAIRY — Like everything else it has become too commercial.

ME — I don't have any objection to the flower and candy people making a buck.

FAIRY — Oh, that's all right. But I was listening to an old geezer on the radio the other day. He was actually pitching an automatic garage door opener as a valentine. That was a bit much.

ME — Fish gotta swim. Birds gotta fly.

FAIRY — What is that supposed to mean?

ME — Simply that the old geezer, as you call him, also has to make a buck. What do you have against old geezers? You're not exactly just off the assembly line yourself.

FAIRY — Let's not let this conversation deteriorate, Buster. I was just wondering why you are so cool toward romance.

ME — I'm not. It's just that I think love and affection are very personal emotions and should be expressed privately. When I was a little kid, I would sometimes send a valentine to a girl I admired, but I was too shy to even sign it.

FAIRY — You, shy?

ME — Terminally. People aren't that way anymore, though. Monday, the Rocky Mountain News will publish an estimated 2,000 valentine wishes in its classified advertising section. Imagine that, 2,000 people going public on such a personal matter.

FAIRY — Some of those are outrageous, but I wouldn't miss reading it.

ME — Remember the one last year that went, "Bananas are yellow, apples are red. You are the most in a waterbed."

FAIRY — That was in the newspaper?

ME — And then there was, "Roses are red, sweet as wine. I wish your pajamas were next to mine. Don't be embarrassed, don't turn red. I meant on the clothesline, not in bed."

FAIRY — Doesn't someone check those out before they are printed?

ME — Sure, but when you are dealing with that many, a few dandies are bound to slip through. There's always a slug of them telephoned in just before deadline.

FAIRY — I'll bet you've got one in there.

ME — Yes. I wrote it just for you.

FAIRY — I can hardly believe that, Buster. How sweet! You see, you are just an old softy after all. What does it say? Do I have to wait until tomorrow?

ME — Roses are red, violets are blue. If I am an old geezer, you are too.

FAIRY — That's my valentine? Well then I've got one for you.

ME — I'll just bet you do.

FAIRY — Lilies are white, carnations are pink. You're lucky I don't hit you with the kitchen sink.

February 13, 1983

Snuggle dancing makes you swoon

TACTILE.

"Hi ho, and good evening, ladies and gentlemen. From El Patio Ballroom, overlooking beautiful Lake Rhoda at Denver's Lakeside

Park, it's music out of the night with Ted Weems and his orchestra, featuring the romantic vocal stylings of Perry COMO!"

I'm just gettting in practice for the series of big-band radio remote broadcasts that are sure to follow the resurgence of ballroom dancing in America. How about this: "Here's that band again! A pleasant good evening, everyone. From the lovely Trocadero Ballroom at Denver's beautiful Elitch Gardens, it's Dick Jurgens and his music!"

I figure that if all the people taking classes in ballroom dancing ever learn to dance without moving their lips, there will be a great demand for radio announcers who know how to work big-band remotes. There are not many of us left. Starr Yelland is the only other one I can think of.

I hadn't realized ballroom dancing was making a comeback until I discovered that a half-dozen or so of our young reporters are learning ballroom dancing in classes offered by Denver Free University.

I don't know if anyone is teaching the East High Hop, a dance popular at all high schools when I was worrying about whom I should ask to the prom. The boy and the girl sort of danced at right angles to each other. She faced the right side of his body and placed her head on his right shoulder.

This side-saddle approach looked better than my description indicates. Actually, it was very sexy, although the word "sex" was not used in mixed company in those days.

It must have been back in the "Happy Days" 1950s that conventional ballroom dancing declined in favor of the free-form, everyone-on-his-or-her-own style of terpsichorean calisthenics popular today.

I never understood why traditional ballroom dancing was abandoned for 20 years. I always looked upon it as socially acceptable public snuggling.

For those who had to look up the word "snuggle," it is a tactile relationship between boy and girl once thought to be pleasurable. I know how naive that appears in times when the likes of Hugh Hefner and other voyeurs have taken all the sweet mystery out of male-female relationships.

There is some irony in the return to popularity of ballroom dancing. What are all these new dancing fools going to use for ballrooms? Remember how upset we all were when they tore down the historic Trocadero? The old Rainbow Ballroom has been remodeled into something else. Ballrooms everywhere have met the same fate.

Perhaps there will be a supply to meet the demand, and new

ballrooms will be built. They ought to be spacious enough for dipping, breaking, spinning, twirling and bending, and also for the adventurous to do the "shag" and the "Suzie Q."

Let me know when they are ready. I'll be out in the garage practicing my radio remote broadcast style. "From high atop the glamorous Interocean Hotel, overlooking the Morey Mercantile warehouse in lower downtown Denver, here are Ace Brigode and his Virginians to ask the toe-tapping musical question, 'Who's Sorry Now?' "

April 9, 1985

Prom wallflower is back in style

DARK SUIT.

There has been a return to elegance in high school proms. Tacky blue jeans and granny gowns are out for the time being. Kids today want a taste of the good life when they go out on the year's major social event.

A boy who works up his courage to pop the prom question these days had better be ready to shell out at least $100, probably more. Rental formal wear will be anywhere from $46 to $50. Dinner for two costs at least $30. Corsages — roses mixed with carnations — run anywhere from $7.50 to $15. And if a boy is a real sport, he'll throw in with a couple of other guys and rent a limousine at $30 an hour.

In my day, we all had something called "the dark suit." Mine was a double-breasted, blue-green chalk stripe. It was a multipurpose garment, suitable for weddings, funerals, commencement exercises, senior proms and other somber occasions.

I hated proms, largely because I was a lousy dancer. My mother did her best to equip me with proper social graces when I was in junior high. She packed me off to a dancing class in some lady's rumpus room. But it didn't work. I just didn't go. Skeeter Bribach and I would hang around Wash Park until we thought the lesson was over and then go back home.

I paid for it by the time I was in high school when everyone was doing the East High Hop, a form of ballroom dancing in which the girl rode sidesaddle. I couldn't dip, spin, twirl or even dance backwards.

My style was more military. I sort of marched, keeping tempo by counting cadence. I never learned to dance without moving my lips.

And so when it came time to line up prom dates, I was avoided like a bastard at a family reunion. I didn't blame the girls, though. Who would want to go to a prom with someone who couldn't dip, spin and twirl, and who whispered "One, two, three — one, two, three," all the time?

My approach was admittedly negative. I'd walk up to some cute little dolly wearing what was then called a "torso dress" and ask, "Hey, you don't want to go to the prom with me, do you?"

I'd get right down to the week before the prom without a date. About the time it appeared my procrastination would pay off, my mother would get a telephone call from the mother of a girl who hadn't been asked to the prom. Playing matchmakers, the two mothers set us up.

I would go through with the charade of calling the girl on the telephone and asking her to go to the prom. She would feign surprise and accept. And so the two wallflowers trudged off to the dance and tried to act as though they were having a good time.

To compensate for my poor dancing skills, I would order a corsage much larger and more expensive than the rest. Since it more nearly resembled a centerpiece at an Eastern Star luncheon, the poor girl never knew whether to pin it on, wear it on her wrist or chase it under the porch with a stick.

She and I would politely say goodnight to each other on her front porch. She couldn't wait to get inside, and I couldn't wait to go home. Not so much as an obligatory kiss.

Painful prom memories.

May 29, 1984

Democracy can't stop terrorism

THE PLAY.

In his book "The Little Drummer Girl," John le Carre makes the point that terrorism is theater. "Theater should be useful. It should make people share and feel. It should, well, waken people's awareness."

Those where the words of Charlie, a young actress, lured into the "theater of the real" by Israeli intelligence to infiltrate a Palestinian terrorist organization. "Do not confuse our play with entertainment," she is told. "When the lights go down on the stage, it will be nighttime in the street. When the actors laugh, they will be happy, and when they weep they will very likely be bereaved and broken-hearted. And if they get hurt — and they will — they will surely not be in a position, when the curtain falls to jump up and run for the last bus home."

America's actors on the stage of the Beirut theater of the real can't jump up and take the last bus home either. We don't know when the final curtain will fall on our unfortunate involvement in Lebanon. We only know that the Islamic Holy War terrorists are planning further suicide attacks against the U.S. presence in the Middle East.

For the third time, the U.S. Embassy in Beirut has been attacked by suicide bombers and more American lives have been lost. The Democrats, sorely in need of a campaign strategy, are trying to make the incident an issue.

A case can be made that American policy under President Reagan in Lebanon is flawed and that we shouldn't have involved ourselves there in the first place. But we must come to understand that a democratic society has little defense against terrorists.

We simply are not willing to pay the price. We refuse to get down in the gutter and fight them at their level. There are still those who believe that eliminating poverty, injustice and other legitimate grievances will somehow remove the cause for terrorism. There is no evidence to support this.

Terrorism succeeds only against free societies. There is no terrorism against Soviet Russia. There was none in Nazi Germany and Fascist Italy. There is rarely terrorism where tyranny is harsh. Terrorism in Ulster is perpetuated because the British are relatively decent to both extremes.

Frantz Fanon, ideologue of the Palestine liberation movement, writes in "The Wretched of the Earth" that violence is a cleansing force, freeing the true believers from inferiority. And in his "Al Fatah's Doctrine," Yehoshafat Harkabi writes: "Violence liberates people from their shortcomings and anxieties. It inculcates in them both courage and fearlessness concerning death."

Free society provides the stage for the drama. Massacres can take place unnoticed in the Third World because the media are not there to report them. But a bomb goes off in Beirut where there are news reporters and TV cameras, giving the terrorists an audience of millions.

Since we are unwilling to deny terrorists that audience and since we refuse to use tyranny to defeat them, we won't soon see an end to the bombings and the killings.

Quote: *The play's the thing wherein I'll catch the conscience of the king.* — From "Hamlet," by William Shakespeare.

September 30, 1984

Patients are the ones who feel a draft

BUNS.

You can tell the difference between patients and people who work in hospitals by whether they are wearing pants. The ones with bare bottoms are the patients. Their uniform is the hospital gown, a shapeless, one-size-doesn't-fit-all garment with two ties in the back, one of which is always broken.

I don't know why, but it is mandatory in all hospitals that before any medical procedure can begin, the patient must be wearing a hospital gown. No cardiopulmonary resuscitation, blood transfusion or other life-saving measure can be administered until emergency room attendants dress the patient in a hospital gown.

"Is he still breathing?" a physician shouts. "Quickly, now! Get him into a hospital gown so we can save his life."

Until I spent a few days in the hospital recently, I had forgotten how obsessed physicians and nurses are with humiliating the ill by dressing them in hospital gowns. It must be something drilled into health care people early in their training.

I have long believed the hospital gown has become an instantly recognizable symbol of subjugation. It is to the patient what the collar is to the slave or the yoke is to oxen. Putting on a hospital gown is the patient's final act of submission to medical authority.

From the patient's standpoint, the hospital gown is useless. It covers only what doesn't need to be covered and leaves the rest to flop, swing, dangle and otherwise be exposed. Males and females alike are vulnerable to the indignity it visits upon them.

I suppose it is practical from the standpoint of the nurses. Since most inoculations are administered smack dab in the old *gluteus maximus*, the hospital gown leaves it always accessible. It is more than accessible, it is actually on display.

While waiting for an X-ray once, I saw a distinguished appearing woman in her middle years rise from a chair in the waiting room when summoned by the technician. She walked majestically into the X-ray room, completely unaware that her hospital gown had parted, revealing buns as bare as the day she was born.

A cold draft is usually the first indication that the hospital gown does little to sustain personal modesty or comfort. The experienced patient learns to walk with one hand behind, clutching the gown together while trying to manage tubes from all body apertures with the other. It is then he regrets that evolution has taken from him a prehensile tail that could be used to push the nurse call button or open the bathroom door.

As a sleeping garment, the hospital gown doesn't rate very high. As the night wears on and you twist and turn when awakened for blood pressure and temperature checks, the hospital gown knots itself into a noose around your neck, leaving your body naked to shiver under those flimsy hospital cotton blankets.

We have organ transplants, microsurgery, space medicine and miracle drugs. Why is it medical science has been able to conquer so many dread diseases, but it has never been able to design a functional hospital gown?

Quote: *I wasn't really naked. I simply didn't have any clothes on.* — Josephine Baker.

June 6, 1985

If all else fails, go hug yourself

HUGGING.

I had not thought much about psychologist Leo Buscaglia until last week when Judith Martin had some rather unfriendly things to say about hugging in her Rocky Mountain News "Miss Manners" etiquette column.

"You there," she wrote, "all you wonderful, warm, cuddly spreaders of happiness who advocate, and practice, hugging everybody in sight, whether you know them or not, just to make a connection from one human being to another — Miss Manners has a small request for you.

"Please keep your hands to yourself or she will call the police."

As I read that, I thought she must have had an encounter with

Ph.D. Buscaglia, known everywhere as the Prince of Hugs. I could just imagine the two of them at some kind of literary cocktail function. Like a nimble cutting horse, Buscaglia tries determinedly to separate Miss Manners from the rest of the herd.

She moves. He moves. Miss Manners is no easy mark, though. She is clever and resourceful, matching Buscaglia step-for-step. Finally, he manages to back her into a corner. She is trapped. Triumphantly, he gives her one of his famous portly hugs, brushing as he does, his whiskered face against her Oil-of-Olayed cheek. Her rigid, frigid body does not yield, but she loses the game anyhow. And worst of all, her hair is mussed.

Is her aversion to social embracing a longstanding one? I found no reference to it in "Miss Manners' Guide to Excruciatingly Correct Behavior." That's her bulky volume on proceeding in life from birth to death in an orderly fashion without making a single false move. She goes on and on about handshaking and kissing, but there is nothing about clasping friend and foe alike in a gesture of friendship and/or love.

That's why I think Miss Manners and Buscaglia have somehow recently met. "And well-meaning or not," she added in her column, "inflicting intimacy on people who don't want it is unspeakably rude, not to mention contemptuous of their feelings."

And then she wrote, "But now we have various mental health propagandists advocating promiscuity in social hugging. . . ." That just has to be our Leo, a man who attributes spiritual power to the act.

Buscaglia, by the way, is to be one of the speakers at a "Dimensions of the Mind" symposium Saturday at the Regency Hotel, sponsored by the Mile Hi Church of Religious Science. I am sure he will, as he always does, reach out and touch not just someone, but everyone.

I am not curious enough to attend. I get my fill of Buscaglia on Channel 12. And, besides, I have the same suspicion of symposia as I do of seminars, clinics, workshops and other events that are thinly disguised methods of separating me from my money.

But I wish Buscaglia no harm. He will pack the joint with his adoring fans. They will go away from the experience the better for it. I don't argue with love in any form. It beats the alternative all hollow.

Quote: *Hugs are good, they feel nice, and if you don't believe it, try it.* — Leo Buscaglia.

November 8, 1983

Psy-cool-ogy

THINK COOL.

I have always thought beer drinkers make a big mistake when they just slam it down on a hot day. When the mercury is up in the mid-90s, beer ought to be consumed slowly and lovingly.

A cold glass of beer is a visual delight. There is so much pleasure in just watching that golden liquid tumble into a frosted glass or mug. Moisture condenses on the outside. Rivulets form crooked little paths that make their way to the bottom of the glass.

The bubbles are fascinating. They seem to come from nowhere. How quickly they race each other to form a creamy collar of foam at the rim of the glass.

A cold glass of beer is enjoyed three times. There's anticipation. When waves of heat shimmer up from concrete and asphalt, thoughts are easily dominated by the idea of cold beer. Realization is next. There is the pleasant little chill as the hand first contacts the glass. Raise the beer to the light. Study its mystery.

Before the glass touches the lips, a moment should be taken to cherish the bouquet. There is something about the smell of malted barley that is honest and straightforward.

It conjures up visions of rolling fields of gently waving grain. There is a tall silo against the horizon, and if you listen closely, you will hear the distant song of a meadowlark from somewhere in the blue and empty sky.

The first sip is quite special. The foam is cool and promising. There is a lovely, ephemeral texture to it. But it only foreshadows the ecstasy to come.

The icy stream slides quickly through the foam and into the mouth. As it lingers there, thirst is drenched. It is slaked. It is soaked. Quenched. Thirst is no more.

Lordy!

The memory of that moment. It is the third time a single glass of cold beer is enjoyed. It sustains one until the next time. Almost.

Beer is not the only cooling thought during these searing days. Let your mind take you across a frosty stubble field in late October.

The air is bracing and there is an explosion of wings as a big rooster pheasant whistles through the air and into the next field. It is autumn, and the wind is cold against your face.

Or when you think cool is your memory locked away in an old fruit cellar under Grandma's farm home? When the door creaked open, you could smell the past.

It was dusty down there. There were cobwebs and old Coleman lanterns. Rusty hand tools were on the walls and there were cardboard boxes filled with memories.

The rough pine shelving along the wall opposite the single window was filled with Mason jars. The labels were hand-lettered. Grape Jel. Watermelon Pickles. Peach Conserve. Wild Plum Butter. Chili Sauce.

And in that cool cellar, you could remember the September afternoon when that chili sauce was simmering in the big iron pot on the stove. You couldn't wait until it was ready.

Thinking cool doesn't have to be in the past. It can be the muslin-covered pillow that waits for you tonight at the top of your bed. It can be arching your body into a secluded mountain pool.

It is cool along Glacier Creek. The water is clear. Lean over, cup your hand and quickly capture just a little to drink. Watch the water bugs skip across the beaver ponds in the mountain meadows.

There is coolness in the shade of the old cottonwood. Lie there in the grass. Be very still. Let the breezes find you and comfort you.

And don't forget the beer.

July 8, 1980

Cheering fades, but party goes on

SAN FRANCISCO — THE ELDERLY WOMAN WAS SITTING ALONE IN THE CHEF'S Table room of the Hilton Hotel. She was drinking white wine and listening to music played on a baby grand piano by a woman wearing a black blouse with silver sequins.

The chant "Jesse! Jesse! Jesse!" occasionally intruded into the room from a TV set in an adjoining bar.

But the elderly woman with the red, white and blue ribbon around her neck didn't seem to hear. Her hair was recently tinted and freshly sprayed. She was humming along with the piano music, a richly ornamented version of the old pop song, "Love is Blue."

"I love it! I love it!" she said in a husky, almost theatrical voice. "My God, I love it. Van Cliburn wrote that, didn't he? I love classical music because it's so, so . . . classical."

"I'd rather have Franklin Roosevelt in a wheelchair than Ronald Reagan on a horse," Jesse Jackson's voice could be heard from the next room.

She took another generous sip of wine.

"I was with the Democrats in New York, but San Francisco is so much better," she said, throwing her head back and laughing. "So many more cocktail parties, so many more receptions! And do you know something, this is my birthday."

The pianist smiled as Jackson's voice intruded once again, "If in my high moments . . ."

Waiters began to fidget, even though they were trying not to notice the woman. The music was now "All the Things You Are." At first, the woman hummed along with the melody. "Tah, tah, tah tah tah tah tah tah tah."

And then she added the words she could remember, "You are the promised kiss of springtime . . ."

"Please forgive me," Jackson's voice implored.

"My compliments to the chef," the woman said even though she had not eaten. "Absolutely terrific," she said, turning again to the pianist. "You play everything from the classics to the . . . well, the classics."

Jackson's voice seemed louder by then. "We must all come up together!" he shouted as roars of approval punctuated his speech.

"Do you know 'When They Begin the Begin'?" she asked as she began to hum the melody for the pianist. "You're getting better with age, my dear. Tah, Tah, Tah, Tah, Tah, Tah Tah Tah Tah Tah."

Long, sustained applause came from the TV set in the bar. The woman's head began to nod as the pianist started to play "Two Guitars." Then she slumped over and went sound asleep. The pianist played more softly then. She finished the song, got up and quietly walked through the door to the kitchen.

The TV in the bar had been turned down by then and the room was very quiet. Two young men and an older woman talked in whispers at a nearby table.

The woman awakened, got up unsteadily and walked toward the door. Just as she got to the two plastic potted palms that flanked the entryway, she turned and said to no one in particular, "No, I'm not going to eat anything for awhile, I'll wait. There are more cocktail parties, more receptions, more . . ."

Her voice trailed away, and she was gone.

July 22, 1984

America needs Iacocca in charge

STUPES.

Gov. Richard D. Lamm's idea of giving the Democratic vice presidential nomination to Chrysler's Lee Iacocca is a good one, but it doesn't go far enough. The Democrats should nominate Iacocca for the top job.

Actually, Lamm would like to see Sen. Gary Hart get the No. 2 spot if Walter Mondale is nominated. If Hart backs out, Iacocca is Lamm's choice for the vice presidential nomination.

People used to look at Richard Nixon and ask, "Would you buy a used car from this man?" Now they are looking at Iacocca and buying his new cars by the bushels. That says something about his economic know-how in one of the world's most competitive industries.

The last time Americans were toying with the idea of making an automobile executive our president was in 1968. George Romney might have been elected instead of Richard Nixon had he not confessed to being "brainwashed" by the Pentagon on Vietnam.

OK, so the country wasn't ready for Romney's candor in 1968. But it sure could use a dose of Iacocca's straight talk about our deficit in 1984. Example: "When you have a deficit of $200 billion and your defense budget is $325 billion, you're keeping the economy going by borrowing money from somebody and turning it over to (Defense Secretary Caspar) Weinberger to spend. And it's not productive. It doesn't do anything. It doesn't provide a service."

What does it do? "I don't know what the heck we get. . . . Everytime I bring it up, someone says it's too classified to talk about. I watched what was paid to Chrysler's former tank division and it makes me want to throw up . . . $490 for a claw hammer. They look like stupes!"

Iacocca denies he has political ambitions. He speaks of the presidency in terms we don't hear from politicians.

"I wouldn't want to try it down there. I've had enough trouble here. . . . Whether it's Reagan or Mondale, the morning after the election, whoever's got it ain't got himself a plum. Man, he's got a problem. I don't envy him being the president because there are some bullets to bite. A lot of them."

There has been very little bullet biting by Democrats or Republicans. We have supplemental appropriations, revenue enhancement, advance budget spending authorization and a lot of other governmental red-ink doublespeak.

It is not the nature of government to be decisive. The bureaucracy postpones decisions, evades reality, submerges truth. With a blunt activist like Iacocca in the Oval Office, we might have a shot at cutting down the superdeficit, reforming antitrust laws, doing something about our trade imbalance with Japan, creating jobs and revitalizing our basic industries.

Offhand, I can't think of any politicians who have lived in the real profit-and-loss world, had real jobs and were paid money for what they actually produced. There is nothing quite like the opportunity of failure to sharpen one's taste for biting bullets.

Quote: *There is a myth that government can do the job cheaply because it doesn't have to make a profit.* — E.S. Savas.

June 24, 1984

Streetwise wildlife gains hold

EAGER BEAVERS.

What? Bambi, Thumper, Flower, Bucky — that crowd, all here? Yes. If you think there is great conflict between wildlife and city life, take a close look at Bear Creek, Clear Creek and the South Platte River. Peek under the floors of deserted shacks or poke around in neglected piles of smelly garbage.

We are not displacing cuddly forest animals by urban sprawl. The little fuzzies actually thrive in the big city and may even take over. This has been obvious for some time to people who live along metropolitan Denver waterways.

The beavers are back along Bear Creek in southwest Denver, and the industrious little rascals are cutting down trees, building dams and producing more beavers.

"We took 120 beavers out of Denver, Lakewood and Wheat Ridge last year, and we didn't even put a small dent in their population," said Jerry Brinker, trapper for the Colorado Agriculture Department.

"The only people authorized to take beaver in the metropolitan area are trappers from the Division of Wildlife and the Agriculture Department. But regulations in Denver and Lakewood make it almost impossible."

Brinker explained that both cities have passed ordinances prohibiting use of traps that cause pain or discomfort to wild animals. "There is no trap that doesn't cause some pain or discomfort. A lot of misguided animal lovers don't understand the meaning of wildlife management. They think they are environmentalists and conservationists, but they aren't.

And so, nature lovers, beavers and other streetwise wildlife are working their way along the South Platte to the very center of Denver. "On the Platte River Greenway, beavers are cutting down trees almost as fast as they are being planted. They particularly love cottonwoods and willows, both in abundance along city waterways.

"These little animals use rivers the way humans use freeways. You would be surprised at the variety of wild animals we have right here in the city. There are deer, coyote, fox, muskrat, prairie rattlesnake, raccoon, squirrels of all kinds, cottontails and jack rabbits, prairie dogs, pheasant and even an occasional bobcat."

Wildlife species rapidly learn to live in harmony with human city dwellers. "The red fox adapts superbly to urban life," Brinker said. "We create skunk and coon habitats with our junk piles and shacks that have floors built off the ground. Our garbage provides a food source.

"Urban areas in Colorado are actually supporting more wildlife than some of the wilderness areas. The greatest wild animal concentration in the metropolitan area is around Chatfield Reservoir. Any greenbelt area attracts animals, however."

Sometimes the wildlife are in conflict with people, Brinker noted. "Many of these animals carry a highly infectious disease called tularemia. It is spread by insects and may be passed on to man. It is not fatal, but it can cause liver damage."

Th . . . Th . . . That's all folks!

May 12, 1983

Big on warm fuzzies

PARENTING.

I hate that word. I don't think you are supposed to make gerunds out of nouns. A gerund is really a verbal noun, not a nounal noun, if there is such a thing.

Still though, it is tough to come up with a single word that describes the act of being a parent. Today I parent. Tomorrow I shall parent. Often I have parented. Boy, have I ever!

I have parented four times. I was parenting long before the sociologists invented the word. I enjoy writing about it, even though I am lacking in any academic credentials. Think of me as a sort of Dr. Spock without portfolio. My advice costs nothing, and that is often what it is worth.

Experience must have some value, though. As noted here before, wisdom always seems to come late. Too late.

I thought about that the other day as I watched a young woman and her crying child in the supermarket. It was a little boy. He appeared to be about 3. She was in a hurry.

She kept shouting at him and jerking his arm. It was "No, don't do this!" and "No, don't do that!" Finally, he just fell down on his knees and refused to walk with her anymore.

She picked him up and put him in the shopping cart, telling him to "shut up" or she was going to spank him. That's about all I could watch. I was embarrassed for her and sorry for the abused child. I walked away.

I want to believe the mother was just having one of those bad days. Maybe she doesn't treat her son that way all the time. We all overreact every now and then.

The episode reminded me of how most of us are guilty of raising our children in a negative environment. We don't do it deliberately. It is the sort of thing that starts about the time the child begins to crawl and reach for the breakables on the coffee table.

From that point on, the child is hemmed in by negatives. Parents, for the best of reasons, begin the endless process of trying to protect their valuables and keep the child from hurting himself.

The thing we forget is to balance all those negatives with positives.

When things go well, we are more likely to say nothing than to reward good behavior with some kind of positive sign of approval.

A lot of people actually do a better job of training their pets than they do of raising their children. A dog gets an ear scratched for retrieving a ball. A child is expected to do the right thing as a matter of course.

It would be interesting to keep track of how often parents say "no" to their children in comparison to "yes." I have no idea, but if memory serves accurately, I was guilty of about a 10-to-1 ratio of "no" to "yes."

The problem is lack of awareness. We react instantly to a negative situation. We often overlook the positive things. By the time a child makes it through the first six years of life, he pretty well knows what he can't do, but not much time has been spent teaching him what he can do. He is left to conclude that good behavior is the absence of bad behavior. That, in itself, is negative.

If I were starting out in the parenting game again, I think I would remind myself each day to watch my child very carefully for the good things. Sure, I would continue to correct bad behavior, but I would try harder to reinforce the good.

The problem with young parents is they are so busy. They are preoccupied with money problems, the usual domestic adjustments, their own emotional needs and a lot of other things. And in all of this, the subtle little good things their children do go unnoticed.

Awareness is the key.

August 23, 1981

Underwear blues

DESIGNER SKIVVIES.

I agree with Andy Rooney that dishes, soap and underwear ought to be white. But now the Jockey® people offer briefs that are blue, like denim jeans.

Joslins had an advertisement in the News Wednesday announcing the briefs are "20 percent off." Judging from the picture, they looked to be more like 85 percent off the guy who was wearing them.

"If you're a denim dude underneath it all," the ad copy says, "you'll cotton to the comfort of Jockey® Jeans Briefs."

I never thought I'd live to see the day when men's underalls looked like their overalls. These are so authentic in appearance that they have contrasting orange stitching. For the sake of comfort, I hope the Jockey® people had the good sense to simulate the copper rivets.

I noticed the Jockey® label no longer is in the back waistband. It is outside, in front and on the left where the thigh bone is connected to the hip bone.

This trademark-flaunting will no doubt prompt the Izod® people to come out with a line of skivvies with a little crocodile on the front. Imagine having to drop your britches just to prove you are a preppie.

Like so many other things these days, we are given more choices in underwear design than we need. Some styles have become more frivolous than functional.

I learned this the hard way. I bought a three-pack of Jockey® shorts not long ago. I guess I thought they were all the same. But when I put on a pair the next morning, I discovered they had no vent. Since I was dressing in the dark, I thought at first I had them on backward.

Closer examination disproved this. There was no vent at all. I concluded that either there had been a critical manufacturing flaw, or that they were designed for short-time wear only.

A lot of men's underwear advertising is slanted toward the woman. This must be the reason Jockey® uses Baltimore Orioles pitcher Jim Palmer to model its shorts.

It is typical of today's permissive society that we talk so openly of undergarments. It used to be that a girl was well past the age of puberty before her mother let her look at the men's section of the Monkey-Ward catalog.

Men also were very sensitive on the subject. I remember an incident confirming this back in 1952. It involved just-elected President Dwight D. Eisenhower and Bal Swan, a friend and prominent Denver banker. The two were frequent fishing companions at Swan's ranch near Pine, Colo.

I asked Swan if he planned to attend Eisenhower's inauguration. "Heck no," Swan replied. "I have seen Ike many times in his underwear on fishing trips. I don't need to go all the way back to Washington, D.C., to see him in a coat with tails and a top hat."

A couple of days later, I was babbling away on the radio, and I told the story as an anecdotal sidelight to the inauguration. It seemed harmless at the time.

I bumped into Swan several weeks later. He didn't speak. As a matter of fact, he didn't speak to me for the next two years. I couldn't figure out what was wrong since we had been friends a long time.

A mutual acquaintance later told me Swan was greatly embarrassed. I suppose he felt I had betrayed a confidence, or even worse, conjured up in the public mind an image of a great war hero and president standing there in his underwear.

September 10, 1981

Tell the trainee that Geno's here

EXPERIENCE.

How it was determined I'll never know, but somehow I have been designated the customer on whom trainees learn their skills. It doesn't matter what sort of service I require, I get the kid who is just starting.

Traineeship, it's called. Don't bother to look it up. There is such a word. A more descriptive term for on-the-job training, however, might be Russian roulette.

I suppose people who enter service careers have to practice on someone, but why me? When a supervisor spots me standing in line, he sends for the new guy. "Quick, go get the trainee. Let him make his mistakes on old Geno," the boss says. "He won't know the difference."

It always happens when I'm in a hurry. If I run into a short-order restaurant for a quick bite, I am the new waitress's first customer. "Ham, scrambled, hash browns, white toast, black coffee," I tell her.

"How do you want your eggs," she responds.

"Scrambled."

"Whole wheat toast?"

"No. White."

"Cream for your coffee?"

"Black."

"How about some ham this morning?"

"That will be fine. Listen, I'm in kind of a hurry . . ."

Forty minutes later, she comes back to my table. She is carrying a Belgian waffle, topped with whipped cream and a little paper Japanese parasol stuck in a maraschino cherry. I hate maraschino cherries.

The banking industry must not pay its tellers very well. There is tremendous turnover in the teller game. I don't believe I have ever had the same one twice.

The problem with drive-up banking, you can't be sure who the teller is. Trying to save time, I make out my deposit slip and endorse the checks in advance. I pick the line that seems to be moving the fastest. But just as I pull up to the customer bay, the bank slips a trainee behind the desk.

I put the checks, deposit slip and my driver's license into the container and send it whooshing through the tube. My gasoline gauge is just one millimeter above the empty mark.

"Are you Gene Am-oh-LEE or Frank Eugene Am-oh-LEE junior?" asks the voice on the little squawk box.

I don't bother to correct the pronunciation of my name. I'm in a hurry and I am running out of gasoline. "I am both," I answer.

"You am both?"

"Yes. Frank E. Am-oh-LEE is my legal name, as you will note on my driver's license, but I go by Gene Amole, I mean, Am-ho-LEE," I answer, not wishing to further complicate matters.

Just as my car runs out of gas, the container comes whooshing back through the tube. When I open it, the slip shows I have withdrawn $200 instead of depositing it. There is no $200 however, but there is a driver's license. The name is not Frank E. Am-ho-LEE. It is Eloy Martinez.

I'm fighting back. I am having a little badge made up. I will wear it on the lapel of my coat at all times. It says:

"Customer Trainee."

November 20, 1983

Locker room fete without a Ripple

BUBBLY.

Lightweight mobile television equipment now permits us to watch the celebration in the winning baseball team's locker room. Happy players, coaches and trainers pour champagne on each other's heads.

Why don't they drink it? With something as expensive as champagne, it seems a shame to just pop the cork and then pour it on the head as though it were Vitalis. Let us imagine instead the San Diego Padres in a more genteel celebration of winning their first National League pennant. Steve Garvey is talking to Rich Gossage.

"Goose, *a votre sante!* This Dom Perignon is superb. I am reminded of the 1973 vintage. Straw color. Excellent nose. Something like the aroma of fresh bread."

"Precisely, Steve. Seventy-three. A very good year. That was also the year the Oakland A's beat the New York Mets four games to three. Reggie Jackson powered the A's to a 3 to 1 win in the seventh game."

"The wine was a Mumm's Cordon Rouge *brut.* The bubbles were mere pin points! But I am told it was not up to 1959."

"That was a really great year. Sandy Koufax, Don Drysdale and the Los Angeles Dodgers put away big Ted Kluszewski and the 'Go-Go' White Sox four games to two. They also put away 15 cases of Moet et Chandon, a noble champagne indeed, but not comparable to the 1929 wines."

"Hardly. Not only was 1929 the vintage year of the century, it was also the year Connie Mack's Philadelphia A's beat the Cubbies four games to one. Jimmy Dykes led all hitters with a .421, followed by Mickey Cochrane's .400. Jimmy Foxx had a respectable .350, but was intentionally passed in the final game. Most Valuable Champagne (MVC) was Piper Heidsieck *demi-sec.*"

"The A's and the Cubs also met in the 1910 autumn classic, and with the same result — four games to one in favor of Philadelphia."

"Yes, but 1910 was not a good wine year. All of August and the first two weeks of September were cloudy. The grapes never fully matured, but the Taittinger *sec,* if somewhat naive, was really not all that bad. There was a bit more sunshine in the Reims area. I see Tony Gwynn is sipping his champagne from a tulip-shaped glass."

"That's Tony for you. He says the bubbles last longer because the wine isn't exposed to as much air. Notice his stance. Tony doesn't choke up on the glass. He holds it by the stem so his hand doesn't warm the wine."

"Why does Garry Templeton still use the flat, shallow glass?"

"Oh, you mean what the French call the *coupe*? Gary is an incurable romantic. He prefers his *blanc de blanc* in a *coupe* because legend has it the artist, Antoine Watteau, designed the glass after a mold he had taken of Marie Antoinette's breast."

"Was she a lefty or a righty?"

"Apparently she could switch."

"Well, here we are almost at the bottom of the bottle. There's just enough bubbly for one more drink. Hold out your glass."

"No, why don't you just go ahead and give me a high-five and pour the rest on top of my head."

October 9, 1984

Oh pain, oh agony

THE BUG.

It is going around. Is it ever! It is also going up, through, down and diagonally. It devastates the mind, the body and the human spirit.

You know you have the bug when your whole being unexpectedly is engulfed by wave after wave of nausea. Then comes the pain. Everything hurts — your hair, your fingernails and your underwear.

It happens so quickly. There you are, maybe driving along the Valley Highway. You are feeling fine. And then, pow!

The first thing to do is to clamp your teeth together. The idea is to keep what's inside from coming outside. Find a park. Crawl behind a bush and try to die.

If that doesn't work, go home. Attempt to deal rationally with your illness. Throw yourself on the bed and sob uncontrollably.

You can take aspirin for your splitting headache. It won't stop the pain, but it will certainly make your ears ring, and ring and ring some more.

Then comes the fever. Why is it when the body gets hot you feel cold? Let your body temperature rise above 100 and there's no way to keep warm.

The thing to do is to put on some wool socks, thermal underwear and your jogging suit. Crawl under a comforter and Grandma's old wool afghan.

Take an electric heating pad with you. Turn the control two clicks to the right. Assume a fetal position around the heating pad. Even so, you will tremble, shiver, shudder, shake and quake.

Do not close your eyes! Please don't close your eyes. If you do, you will run the risk of the very worst kind of disorientation.

It is as though your poor stomach is on a terrifying elliptical course through the void of your agony. It swoops and turns. And then your stomach dives and spins out of control.

Open your eyes before those terrible laser beams start to burn through the brain! Hold onto the pillow so that the bedroom will stop turning.

When sleep finally comes, the terror begins. It was Hamlet, who said, "To sleep: perchance to dream: ay, there's the rub; For in that sleep of death, what dreams may come."

Bizarre dreams, that's what kind of dreams. You will find yourself held captive by a band of squat partisans who talk menacingly of a class struggle.

There is an addled blond woman among them. She carries an old chrome-plated revolver. Her careless handling of it terrifies you and the other prisoners.

And then the awful word comes down. You and the other homely ones are to be banded together and marched off to a device that will turn you into apricots.

You awaken with a start. The clammy feeling is gone. Now you are hot. Burning hot. You are slathered in sweat. You get up and stumble into the bathroom.

Are your kneecaps going to fall off? Your thighs ache and your hands tremble. You reach for the light. It is blinding.

You steady yourself by clutching at the wash basin. Don't look in the mirror! No! That face in the mirror is not you. It is Dorian Gray and he is crumbling to dust.

Your stomach growls, retches, gurgles and contracts. Your lungs are tight with phlegm. You cough until your throat is raw. When you speak, the voice is not human. You sound like Babba Yaga, the Russian witch. That is if you can speak at all.

Damn flu!

March 27, 1980

Born-again taxpayer loves April 15

GOODIES.

Maybe you have noticed that sunny smile on my face. It is because I have changed my opinion about income taxes. No more grumbling. No more breast beating. No more cursing the Internal Revenue Service. I am a Born-Again Taxpayer.

I just can't wait for Friday, April 15. It wasn't always that way. I used to hang around the mailbox at the main post office downtown until just before the midnight deadline to mail my return. I wanted to hold onto my money until the very last minute.

Not now. The sooner my hard-earned dollars get in the government pipeline, the better. That way I can get first shot at all the goodies. Just thinking about it makes me feel like a kid at Christmastime.

There are so many gimmies on my shopping list this year I don't know where to begin. I should start with the Pentagon before the stingy old Congress cuts President Reagan's defense budget.

Choices! I don't know whether to go for the MX missiles in the old silos in this country or the Pershing 2 and cruise missiles in Western Europe.

You are right. There has been some attitude modification on my part. I no longer think of taxpaying as the government taking money from me. We Born-Again Taxpayers regard April 15 as a glorious opportunity to go out and spend.

It's a ball to buy a lot of stuff you have always wanted. I'll take three of those! Wrap up that one! Gosh, I can't decide between those two, so I'll take both!

See how easy it is to get caught up in the buying spirit? Once you get started, it is sometimes difficult to stop.

Central America is a whole bunch of fun. I can either overthrow the government of Nicaragua or I can help keep the El Salvador government from being overthrown. What the heck, I'll do both.

I certainly want to save a few bucks for Mexico. Ready for this? What I think I'll do is send money to Mexico to pay interest on loans it owes our banks so they won't go broke. I just can't pass up a bargain.

I hope I have enough left for a little shopping spree in the Middle East. I definitely want to spend a few bucks to keep our Marines in Lebanon. That way Israel can divert its resources to build more settlements on the West Bank. This will keep tensions high and will ensure that I won't lose the opportunity to spend more money in that area for years to come.

Now don't get the idea I'm going to spend all my dough overseas. No sir. This old boy buys American. If someone doesn't beat me to it, I want to subsidize the tobacco industry so it can continue to create jobs in the cancer field.

Gosh, I hope I have enough left to pay interest on the national debt. It is one of the few instances that you don't have to deduct interest from your income taxes.

Got to keep deficit spending high so interest rates will stay up. That way people won't be able to find jobs and I'll spend more of my money on welfare costs. Generous, huh?

What's money for if it isn't to spend?

April 14, 1983

Junk mail enough to make you AARP

MATURITY.

The American Association of Retired Persons is still trying to put me out to pasture. Just as I had thought I was no longer an involuntary member of the senior citizens lobby, AARP is on my tail again.

You may recall my distress at being made an unwilling member of Rep. Claude Pepper's political action committee. I refuse to belong to any organization I don't willingly join. And even though I am past 60, I have no intention of being exiled to some gawdawful sand dune in Arizona.

As soon as my views appeared in this column, AARP people in Washington advised me in a sharply worded letter that my name has been purged from their membership lists. Peace at last, I thought.

But they are after me again. On an envelope addressed to Frank E. Amole at my address were the words: THERE'S GOOD NEWS — OPEN CAREFULLY. The letter began, "Dear AARP Member:"

It then went on to explain that I can't be refused membership in AARP's Group Hospital Plan, which has increased its benefits again at no increase in price. I believe it. If I can't refuse membership in AARP, I'll certainly have a tough time staying out of its Prudential insurance program.

I don't know why Executive Director Cyril F. Brickfield wasn't told of my resignation. I don't pay dues, go to meetings, attend potlucks or square dances, nor do I participate in any way. Now AARP says I can't be kept out of its insurance program.

The next day or so, I got another letter from my old pal, Executive Director Brickfield. This time he wanted me to join the AARP Motoring plan provided by Amoco Motor Club for $24.95 a year. That's less than 7 cents a day, and I get a reflecting bumper sticker.

In the same mail, I got another letter addressed to Gene Amole enclosing my new AARP personalized Medical Identification Card (CAB 0337462). This time it wants $13.45 a month from me for its insurance plan and another $8.95 for my wife, Trish.

AARP also is offering me a subscription to its magazine, "Modern Maturity," representation in Washington, D.C., and at the Colorado Legislature, a pharmacy service, a homeowner insurance program, a travel service, a money market trust, a motoring plan and hotel, motel and car rental discounts. My cup runneth over.

But the good news stopped when yet another letter from AARP came to our house. It was addressed to Fugene E. Amolerank. I have no idea who Amolerank is. He must be an old guy, though, since the letter offered him a membership in AARP.

Who do you suppose Amolerank is? You don't think Trish is fooling around, do you? When I leave for work from the front door in the morning, is Amolerank coming in the back door?

"He's gone," Trish is whispering, "Come in, Fugene. He won't be home until 6 o'clock. While you draw the blinds, I'll get the wine and cheese. It's whoopee time!"

Amolerank had better join AARP. If I get my hands on the s.o.b., he'll need all the hospital insurance he can get.

October 11, 1984

Romancing the stone

DIRECT SALES.

"Tom, why is it you are able to sell diamonds for so much less than retail outlets?"

"It's because we have eliminated middleman costs by going direct to the source. I will go anywhere in the world to get diamonds.

"It is sometimes necessary for me to organize safaris and make my way along the Chicapa, Luachimo, Chiumbe and Luembe rivers to the diamond-bearing alluvial deposits in the Kasai region. You have no idea how difficult travel can be in the bush.

"If you somehow manage to make it by the Cuban mercenaries and the Bantu tribesmen, there's the tsetse fly. Tsetse flies everywhere! If you run out of bug spray, baby, you're SOL. You don't find many 7-Eleven stores in Angola.

"Nights in the rain forests can be harrowing. A fire keeps the camp relatively safe, but there's no way to shut out jungle sounds. Can't get a wink of sleep with all that snarling, growling and screeching going on.

"That's not the worst of it. Those insistent, throbbing, pounding drums unnerve the daylights out of you. You don't know what the primitive savages are saying to each other. But after you listen for awhile, it occurs to you that they are meeting for lunch, and you are on the menu.

"I hate it when the guide and bearers panic and run off screaming into the jungle. It is terrifying to be in the bush alone. There's no Bo Derek out there in the real world, Pal.

"Sometimes we have to go to the Kono district of Sierra Leone. Ever been there? Don't go. You have to go down into the Bafi-Sewa River drainage system. Smelly. Is it ever! The snakes are unbelievable.

"I mean, we are talking major league snakes! You don't want to have anything to do with the Gabon viper, or *Bitis gabonica,* as it is also known. Those suckers run up to six feet long. Step on one, and that's all she wrote. I mean, it's the BIG sleep. You don't want a mamba slithering up your leg into your britches, either. I hate snakes. Why does it always have to be snakes?

"I am not crazy about going down in those diamond mines, either. The big one in Tanzania is at Mwadui. It is so dark down there you can't find your you-know-what with both hands. If you've seen one rock, you've seen them all. The foreman is a brutal son-of-a-gun. He's that way because a crazed Arab handyman once boarded up his girl friend.

"Once you get the diamonds, they have to be cut. Your hands get sweaty and shaky. One little mistake in cleaving, and that 58-facet brilliant cut you have been planning is just another pile of dust on the floor.

"And then it's off to Antwerp. Diamond wholesalers are a bunch of bandits. When supply is greater than demand, they squirrel away the surplus to keep prices artificially high. Give me a break!

"Next week I'm off to Brazil. You know what they have down there? They have *Leptotyphlopidae* snakes. Those nasty little devils actually suck out the contents of termites' stomachs. Disgusting! But as I say, we'll go anywhere for diamonds."

"Now, you have a friend in the diamond business."

November 6, 1984

The eternal flame can only be hope

HOPE.

Is there the tiniest detail of John Kennedy's death 20 years ago we haven't touched again, seen again, felt again? Probably not. For those old enough to remember, it has been a poignant and disturbing *deja vu*.

For the young, the event has been frozen in history. It is beyond their reach. They have no memory of the hurt, the emptiness, the fury Americans experienced when their president became a smiling target in the cross-hair sights of the assassin's rifle.

The old questions remain. There are no new insights as we pick away at the absolutes. John Kennedy was gunned down by a young psychopath, who in turn was gunned down by an old psychopath. Violence begat violence, as it always has and always will.

If, as Carl Sandburg wrote, "History is a bucket of ashes," is it too late to stir those ashes for some still-warm embers? Are we too distant from that day in Dallas to remember why we were so profoundly affected by Kennedy's death?

Sure, there are the quick, easy memories of Camelot. The Arthur of this enlightened domain was handsome Jack. His beautiful Jacqueline was queen. There was adorable Caroline. Who can forget brave little John-John? And then there were all those bright young knights in burnished armor to defend the splendid castle.

It wasn't all that way, though. There were the ugly times. Kennedy accepted full blame for the Bay of Pigs fiasco, even though the scheme had been hatched in the preceding Eisenhower administration and was recommended by every member of the Joint Chiefs of Staff.

Although the Cuban missile crisis was perhaps Kennedy's finest hour, his support for the civil rights movement in the South now appears something less than enthusiastic.

Historians will debate whether Kennedy's presidency was one of style or substance. Was it all show or did he set a new American course when he declared: "Let the word go forth from this time and place, to friend and foe alike, that the torch has been passed to a new generation of Americans — born in this century, tempered by war, disciplined by a hard and bitter peace, proud of our ancient heritage and unwilling to witness or permit the slow undoing of those human rights to which this nation has always been committed"?

Rhetoric? Most Americans didn't think so then. There was something about the way Kennedy spoke to us that made us think there was hope. He told us we were the masters of events, not their slaves, and we believed him. That was it, wasn't it? Exactly. He made us believe in ourselves.

Did that belief die in Dallas with John Kennedy? No president since has been able to make us really think that we control our own future. We are overwhelmed with events that push us ever closer to the seemingly inevitable day of nuclear holocaust and "The Day After."

The generation to which John Kennedy's torch was passed could do nothing but stand and cry when its flame flickered out just 20 years ago. The torch is still there, but there are doubts it will ever again be ignited.

Only hope remains.

November 22, 1983

Phlakes Phlee Phlox

CAR-RT SORT.

That's the way the new Springhill planting and seed catalog was addressed to my wife. And right there on the cover was a "MEMO from Jonathan Merriweather."

"Special gift for Mrs. Gene Amole," it began. "We have a very special gift to bring a touch of beauty to your Denver garden and provide the most gorgeous bouquet ever seen in the Amole home — six special deluxe glads. They're yours free! See pg. 2."

Merriweather's catalog couldn't have come at a better time. There are still 18 inches of snow of our award-winning blizzard on my lawn, only it isn't fluffy and white anymore. It has a crust of dirty ice and some frozen dog poo I haven't been able to get to.

Merriweather is the Betty Crocker of the seed and plant game. The drawing of him indicates he is about 60. Nice-looking man with gray hair and mustache. He is smiling, his collar is open, and there are little sun crinkles at the corners of his eyes.

I believe Merriweather exists. I am as sure of that as I am of a real Betty Crocker. I also believe in the tooth fairy and Santa Claus. I do not believe in Sara Lee or Ronald Reagan. Four out of six ain't bad.

Anyhow, I looked on pg. 2, and sure enough, I get six glad bulbs free with an order of $25 or more, "exclusive varieties with exhibition quality blooms."

I have no problem with that. Gee, I want practically everything in the catalog. I will certainly order some Perennial Dragonhead. "Pink trumpets sparkle all up and down the erect 3 to 4 foot stems, blooming continuously from July to September."

I'll want some Creeping Phlox. "Nothing in the garden can beat this winner for the look of a lush, luxurious pastel carpet. No other plant spreads so lavishly, needs little attention, flowers so profusely."

Phantastic! I can't wait until all my phriends and phamily come over to my house to see my phabulous phlox. Those beautiful phlowers will phill my back yard with color. What phun we will have! There are phour or phive colors. And just think, I get six glad bulbs absolutely phree!

Merriweather also recommends Giant Robinson Strawberries. "Largest berries in the world! Huge as golf balls. One giant, bright red strawberry makes a mouthful."

I'll want some Fancy Caladium, Hybrid Freesia, Blue Wisteria Vine, Japanese Toad Lily, Silvermound Artemesia, Dianthus Dana, Knights of the Roundtable Delphinium and Old-Fashioned Bleeding Heart.

What a yard I'll have this year! This is the garden that will send Herb Gundell to the showers. When I look up from my Springhill catalog, I squint my eyes and look out the kitchen window. The dirty snow, ice and frozen dog poo are gone.

My privacy fence is covered with Blushing Maid Climber Roses. Blue hydrangeas are blooming where the ash pit used to be. The back fence is aflame with dwarf Hershey Red Azalea. The patio is shaded by a giant weeping willow.

Early spring phever!

January 25, 1983

How to survive exercise class

The women in charge of aerobic exercise classes were all sired by Marine Corps drill instructors. Richard Simmons is a myth. No one sits cross-legged on the floor, looks into your eyes and lisps that your pounds are going to melt away.

Instead, there is a 98-pound lady with no behind at all. She has the voice of a major league baseball umpire, and she stands in front of a mass of sweating females, hollering: "Bun burn! Bun Burn! Burn those buns!"

I have no explanation for the popularity of this madness. Classes are organized for almost every segment of society. There are even Christian and Jewish exercise groups for those who wish to suffer in the company of others of like spiritual persuasion.

But the size-5 women who run this organized agony are all the same. They are little bits of things with perfect bods. All have a fondness for the insistent tempos of music by Michael Jackson, Berlin, the B-52s and Lionel Richie. The music may turn your mind to yogurt, but if you stick with it, you'll be as strong as Mr. T.

The aerobic exercise game has its own hierarchy. The "jocks," as they think of themselves, are clones of the head lady. They wear head bands, flesh-colored Danskins, belts and leg-warmers. They work out by the mirrors at the head of the class so they can admire their own tiny fannies.

The older women stay at the rear of the room, as far away from the mirrors as they can get. They wear old "Orange Crush" T-shirts and purple leotards to conceal varicosity problems.

"We want those muscles long 'n' lean! Long 'n' lean! Stretch! I mean STRETCH!" she commands. "Come on, ladies, don't die on me!"

But there are times when you think you will die. Then you are afraid you won't. You don't care about lean muscles. You just want Michael Jackson to shut up.

There are several options. Feign a leg cramp, break off the exercise and go to the wall to do a non-violent stretching exercise.

Or when the going gets too heavy, pause to check your pulse. This conveys an impression that you are marching to your own drummer and are really following a rigid and controlled program.

Buy yourself extra time by keeping your jumping rope hopelessly knotted. Act embarrassed as you try to straighten the rope while the others are wheezing through their routines.

Those who are really into exercise avoidance have made an improvement on the old bathroom gambit. Watch from the corner of your eye to see when someone else goes to the biffy. Then you go to the door, discover it is locked, snap your fingers and return to your place. When the occupant leaves, you go again. You have actually doubled the amount of time you have not exercised.

Of course, you can mumble something about having had surgery. Or there is always the time-proven ploy of smiling sweetly and referring to your baby. Take care not to mention your "baby" is a sophomore in high school.

Or better yet, stay home.

October 18, 1983

4

TIME & TIME AGAIN

Once again, Denver gets 'no respect'

CROYSENTS.

Denver's reputation as the Rodney Dangerfield of cities remains alive and well. Yet another visiting journalist has passed through town and has found our level of sophistication wanting. This time we get "no respect" from C.W. "Chuck" Nevius, a sportswriter for the San Francisco Chronicle.

"Denver is the little town that became big, but never grew up," he observed in a column dated Dec. 29, 1984, the day before the Denver Broncos were knocked out of the NFL playoffs by the Pittsburgh Steelers.

"It's all dressed up with skyscrapers and an international airport, but Denver can't keep from tugging at its itchy collar and tight tie.

"At the deli where the sign says, 'Sure, we're open,' you ask the woman what kind of breakfast rolls they have.

" 'Croysents,' she says with a friendly smile.

"A snicker at that point could get you in big trouble out here. If Pittsburgh has to live with the image of steelworkers who wipe their hands on their pants before they shake hands, Denver seems constantly to be denying that there are hitching posts on the main streets."

He then linked our inelegance to Denver's past. "It has always been a problem out here in Sophistication Gap. In the 1880s, Big Jim Tabor made millions mining silver in the hills above Denver, and then built a lavish opera house so he could import the divas from New York. Big Jim went bust, but Denver never did."

That sent us scurrying to history books to learn more about this Big Jim Tabor who figured so significantly in Sophistication Gap's rustic past. There was an Augusta Tabor, a Baby Doe Tabor and a Silver Dollar Tabor, but no Big Jim. Nevius must have been referring to Horace A.W. Tabor.

Nowhere is it recorded that Tabor went by the name of Big Jim, or even Big Horace. Big Horace has an interesting ring to it, though. Anyone calling himself Big Horace during the silver boom would have had to have been big, indeed.

Nevius, who was brought to the Chronicle to cover the Oakland

Raiders only to have them move to Los Angeles, devoted most of his column to the Denver Broncos. He accurately portrayed them as a *raison d'etre* for many of our citizens. I would have gone further. The Broncos have become our state religion — sort of the Father, the Son and the Point After Touchdown.

He apparently avoided big trouble by not snickering at the deli lady, and his column ended on this positive note: "The croissant, by the way, was excellent — light, flaky and delicious. Which is a reminder that sophistication isn't nearly as important as having the right ingredients."

Ah, but it's not the yeast, butter, milk, flour, salt, sugar and eggs that make our "croysents" flaky. The trick is to properly layer cold butter with warm dough.

A little egg wash before baking at 400 degrees for 12 minutes will give the top crusts a nice golden, sophisticated luster.

Quote: *A critic is a man who knows the way but can't drive the car.* — Kenneth Tynan.

January 10, 1985

A matchless story of love played out

SILVER QUEEN.

As the old '27 Dodge lurched along Tenmile Creek, I asked Dad how much longer before we got to Leadville. "Oh, not much," he answered. "Maybe another half-hour or 45 minutes. No longer than that."

It was a warm summer afternoon. Dust swirled behind us as Grandpa talked of long ago when he was a boy and delivered snowball flowers to the fancy Mrs. Tabor. "She was always nice to me and sometimes even gave me a tip," Grandpa said.

I was getting carsick and was only half listening. I wasn't much more than 8 or 9 and couldn't understand why we were driving all this way just to see an old lady who always sat beside her shanty. Grandpa called her "Baby Doe." Why would they call an old lady "Baby"? I wondered.

About the time I got that salty taste in my mouth and was ready to throw up, Dad pulled the car to the side of the dirt road. We got out and started to walk toward some old buildings on bleak Fryer Hill, just east of Leadville. "That's far enough," came a voice up and to the right of us.

Elizabeth McCourt "Baby Doe" Tabor was dressed in rags. A hat was pulled down almost over her eyes. The back of her chair was pushed to the side of the shanty. She was loosely holding an old rifle across her knees.

Dad and I didn't say anything. Grandpa did all the talking. He tried to make her remember who he was, telling her about snowball flowers. They talked of the old times in Denver. She got friendlier but wouldn't let us come any closer. After about an hour, we drove back home.

Five years later, and exactly 49 years ago this past Wednesday, two neighbors, Tom French and Sue Bonney, broke into the shanty and found Baby Doe on the floor, frozen to death. Coroner James Corbett said she probably died two or three weeks earlier. She was 81.

And so ended her long vigil. Baby Doe's husband, the once-wealthy and powerful Sen. H.A.W. Tabor, had told her 36 years earlier on his deathbed to "hold onto the Matchless." The Matchless was an old mine believed by Tabor to hold a mother lode of pure silver.

When the story reached Denver the next day, newspapers published photographs not of the wizened old bag lady who died alone but of the comely young woman who became Horace Tabor's bride in a ceremony attended by President Chester Arthur. Tabor had created a scandal when he divorced his wife, Augusta, to marry Baby Doe.

There was no mother lode in the Matchless. The Tabor fortune was gone. The love story finally played out when Baby Doe was laid to rest alongside her Horace in Mount Olivet cemetery in Denver.

Something else ended on Fryer Hill. The spirit of the early West died along with Baby Doe. She was proud to the end. She had seen the best and the worst of life in her time.

She played by the old rules and never gave up. Her character was hard as flint. Her standards were high. She refused all offers to help. She maintained a quiet dignity until the end. Baby Doe remained constant.

It was the world outside that had changed.

March 8, 1984

Let's remember the 'little people'

YOUTHDAYS.

Leadville was still prosperous in the spring of 1918. Large lead, zinc and manganese deposits were worked profitably to meet the industrial demands of World War I. The town had survived the depression of 1893. The "days of panic and gloom," as the Herald-Democrat called them, were in the past.

But life in "The Magic City" was still hard. The winters were long and cold — so cold that the frozen ground had to be dynamited before the dead could be buried. It was there Annie Tekansik lived all of her 15 years and three months.

Certainly Leadville produced many more prominent and colorful citizens than Annie. There was the heroine of the Titanic disaster, Mrs. J.J. "Unsinkable Molly" Brown. Railroad tycoon David Moffat lived there for a time. Wheeler-dealer Horace A.W. Tabor parlayed a $17 grubstake into a fortune at Leadville.

Perhaps the town's most noted citizen was Elizabeth McCourt "Baby Doe" Tabor, "Haw" Tabor's second wife. When he died April 10, 1899, his last words to her were, "Hold onto the Matchless," a mine he believed still held a fortune. Baby Doe held on until her death in 1935.

The Tekansik family found no mother lode of gold or silver in Leadville. They were the little people about whom historians rarely write. Annie's father worked as a miner and operated a small store at 322 Front St. Annie was born in the back of that building and lived her entire life there.

It was exactly 65 years ago this week that Annie became ill with pneumonia. Her name and her simple story are remembered only because the late Bill Beardshear, a veteran Denver newspaperman, came across a crudely written notice of her death. Obviously moved by it, he pasted a copy in one of his old scrapbooks of clippings.

Judging from an adjoining newspaper obituary, the notice was written by Annie's sister, Mary. Here is its testimony of faith and family love:

"Our daughter and sister — as we like to tell about her. she has been a might good girl. she never wished bad to any body. She was good working girl and husky girl. she like her sisters and brothers. she always was with papa and her mother. and her sisters and brothers liked her well.

"She was a good Catholic girl. she love Church. she loved holy things. she always go to church and pray and she like to go to Communon and Confesion. she wanted holy scapler ... and she wanted prayer beads and everything that is holy. she never go to Dance and balls and those happy places and skating rinks etc. ...

"She used to go see the dead and sick. She never cared for any bad places ... she always loved flowers and all animals and she worked always in kind and in happenes.

"She had limonija which it was black limonija. She was only sick about 15 days. She got sick May 25, 1918, she died twenty minutes to eight tonight. She was 15 years old in Feb. She never love any good cloths. she never swear, she never used bad language.

"She loved everybody in her youthdays."

May 22, 1983

Birthday boy

LENSES AND APPLES.

At some point Thursday, Thomas Hornsby Ferril will be introduced at a public gathering. He will be given a warm round of applause. After all, Tom is Colorado's poet laureate.

He will stand and smile modestly, and then he will make a gracious little speech telling how happy he is to be there. He will conclude by saying, "You have made this occasion very special for me, because today ... well, today is my birthday."

There will be one difference Thursday. I have it on the highest authority that Feb. 25 is his real birthday anniversary. Tom has been known to give that little speech June 18, Nov. 5, Aug. 22, April 29, March 13 and on other dates only he can recall.

There is something inside Tom that makes him announce in public that it is his birthday, even when it isn't — *especially* when it isn't. He has never explained to me why he does this. I suspect it is because there is a lot of little boy in Tom Ferril. That's a good way to be when you turn 86, or 147, if you count all those other birthdays he has claimed.

There is no other American writer I admire more. Tom is incomparable. That is not just my view. Bernard de Voto described him as "the only first-rate poet in the West ... who happens to be one of the best writers of prose anywhere."

Carl Sandburg said of Tom: "He's terrifically and beautifully American. He is a poet, wit, historian, man of books and human affairs, and so definitely one of the Great Companions."

And another Pulitzer Prize winner, Peter Viereck, wrote, "There is one very special emotion that Ferril conveys more movingly, more heart-breakingly than any other poet in American literature; the emotion of wistfulness."

H.L. Mencken was a Ferril fan. He published some of his long poems, including "Magenta," in The American Mercury. In addition to his many books, Tom's work has also appeared in The Atlantic, Harper's, The Saturday Review, Yale Review, The New Yorker, New York Times and Popular Mechanics.

Popular Mechanics? Yes. The same man who wrote "Here is a Land Where Life is Written in Water," the text of the murals in the rotunda of the Colorado State Capitol, also sold an article to Popular Mechanics on how to burglar-proof cellar windows with old tire chains.

That's one of the many reasons Tom is so important to his many friends. He never lets his genius interfere with his humanity. I have never heard him talk down to anyone.

His poems are rich with the imagery of mountains, rivers, the plains and the sky. In his "Time of Mountains," he wrote, *I have held rivers to my eyes like lenses, and rearranged the mountains at my pleasure, as one might change the apples in a bowl.*

But his poetry is not about the natural environment. "Man is the subject of poetry, and man alone," Tom wrote. He loves mountains and rivers, but they are only his tools for implementing life. Ferril never forsakes the play for the setting.

For those who want to know him better, Channel 6 is repeating "Thomas Hornsby Ferril, One Mile Five-Foot-Ten," Thursday at 9:30 p.m. It is a 30-minute television portrait of Tom, a program produced by Don Kinney's Rocky Mountain Reflections production company. It has been shown nationally on the Public Broadcasting System and has received an Emmy.

The program was a labor of love for those who worked on it, and it is their way of telling Tom how much they care for him.

February 25, 1982

Highway history

THE VALLEY.

Some people still call it the Valley Highway. There are other names for that part of Interstate 25 that cuts through Denver. Common decency prohibits their use here, however.

It is one of those city necessities everyone hates but can't live without. Mark Ulysses Watrous, the man who guided the engineering for the Valley Highway, died Monday. He was 88.

The Valley Highway is certainly the most common of Denver's physical urban denominators. It connects the north to the south and separates east from west. It follows the South Platte River valley right through the center of the city.

What was called "Platte Valley Drive Road" was planned in 1938 by the Public Works Administration, one of the many government agencies that sprouted during the administration of Franklin D. Roosevelt.

Another Depression-era agency, the Works Progress Administration, actually built a four-lane highway along the east bank of the South Platte between West Colfax and West 38th avenues in 1940.

The next year, the Colorado Legislature passed what it called a "Freeway Law," the first legal step toward giving the city a non-stop north-south thoroughfare.

When World War II broke out, almost all highway construction came to a halt. The planning went on, however. Charles Vail, then chief engineer of the Colorado Highway Department, managed to keep the Valley Highway plan alive. Before moving to state government, Vail had been a manager for parks and improvements in Denver.

Vail never lived to see the highway. He died in 1944 and the Colorado Highway Advisory Board immediately recommended abandoning the project because of a lack of financing. The cost was then estimated at $14.5 million.

Acting Chief Highway Engineer A.F. Hewitt immediately terminated all planning. There was some talk of alternate north-south routes. Some wanted Broadway. Others suggested Federal, University and Colorado boulevards.

Hewitt couldn't hold onto the job. Enter Mark Watrous. He was managing a construction firm in Pueblo when Gov. John Vivian appointed him to Colorado's top highway job. That was in 1946.

The first thing Watrous did was to reactivate the Valley Highway plan. The war was over and funding for urban highway projects began to trickle down to Denver.

Ground was broken at West 46th Avenue on Nov. 16, 1948. The feisty little Watrous began to make news as Denverites watched with some pride and a lot of amazement as the city's first freeway snaked its way across the city.

The estimated cost jumped to $33 million. More than 500 separate land acquisition deals were made. Sixty-two bridges, overpasses, underpasses and other structures were built under Watrous' watchful eye. Section by section it opened. It seemed there were cars waiting on the ramps to use the highway the minute each part was completed.

There were problems. Drainage was not adequate and some underpasses filled with water even during a light shower. The largest of these concrete flood plains — along the South Valley — was quickly dubbed "Lake Watrous."

Four lanes were completed between West 52nd and East Evans avenues on Nov. 23, 1958. In those days, it took 16 minutes to drive from one end to the other.

There are now as many as eight lanes and it still isn't wide enough. In 1944, it was estimated that a maximum of 108,000 vehicles would use the highway each day. Stan Brown, public relations director for the Highway Department, said there are some days when as many as 170,000 cars use the highway.

The worst intersections are at Interstate 70 and West Sixth Avenue. Brown said there is just no money available to put in the kind of interchanges needed.

January 31, 1980

Listen to rumble, rattle and roar . . .

ALL ABOARD!

Now that the Regional Transportation District is thinking of buying the old Rio Grande Zephyr passenger train, maybe it's time to bring back the Yampa Valley Mail. It wasn't very fast, but it sure was a lot of fun.

The RTD wants to run the nine-coach train, complete with lounge car, between Denver and Longmont. Rio Grande now uses the Zephyr on its Denver-to-Salt Lake City run. That service will halt April 24.

I have no idea if there is sufficient passenger demand to justify fixed-guideway, mass-transit service to Longmont, but Burt Hubbard, our man who covers the RTD, said he has had several calls approving the idea.

A case can be made for bringing back the Yampa Valley Mail, a two-car passenger and freight train that made its last run from Denver to Craig in 1968. Maybe Rio Grande has "Little No. 9," as it was called, stashed away in a roundhouse somewhere.

It was a 2,000-horsepower diesel that could practically climb a wall. Little No. 9 plowed through shoulder-high mountain snowdrifts. Old-timers can remember only one time when "The Little Engine That Could" got stuck. It was in the 1940s when she finally wheezed to a halt at Phippsburg, 22 miles south of Rabbit Ears Pass.

There were many times when the Mail was the only connection between the outside world and people who lived in the Yampa Valley. In the big spring storm of 1957, Little No. 9 was the valley's only source of food.

Before Rio Grande finally got Public Utilities Commission permission to abandon the route, the train made a 232-mile trip every day from Denver through the Moffat Tunnel and down the Yampa River Valley to Craig in seven hours, 29 minutes.

You are thinking that's a long time for a trip from Denver to Craig. And it was, but she had to make a minimum of 20 stops. That's what made riding so much fun.

Everyone knew everyone else. When I was a passenger, the engineer was J.E. Sullivan. Roy James was the fireman. The conductor was C.B. Gray, and the brakeman was M.L. Williams Sr. All were on a first-name basis with almost all the passengers.

Gray was host, candy butcher, raconteur, entertainer. He knew all the gossip. There were reports — never confirmed — that if there was a particularly nice sunset, Little No. 9 would stop for a few minutes so the passengers could watch.

Maybe the Yampa Valley Mail is an idea whose time has come again. Since it passed through both Winter Park and Steamboat Springs, it could be made into a winter sports excursion train.

When service was finally halted, Rio Grande said only 4.7 passengers were using the train daily. The route was losing $300,000 a year. Yampa Valley residents made a big fuss when the PUC held hearings in Denver to stop service.

The hearing room was jammed with folks from Craig, Steamboat Springs and the other 37 communities along the line. But there was only one problem.

They all *drove* to Denver.

March 24, 1983

Endurance run

THE ROMANCE.

It has gone out of commercial flying. The planes are too long, too wide, too crowded. The old sense of excitement isn't there anymore.

Women passengers used to dress up to take a trip. They wore suits, blouses, heels, hose, Chantilly perfume and little pill-box hats with net veils that came down to the nose. And there was the obligatory gardenia corsage.

Now, the idea now is to dress as though you were going to clean the garage.

Families came out to the airport to see off loved ones. Sometimes they would get on the plane and spend a few moments with the departing passenger to share a small part of the adventure.

The planes were slower. There was time to fantasize about the stewardesses. You could tilt back the big comfortable seats and read almost an entire book on a flight from Denver to New York. The old piston engines were nice. Their steady drone was like a narcotic. Some people believed they could sleep better on a DC-6 than they could at home.

It was nice to wander up and down the classless aisles and exchange big talk with the other passengers. There was something about commercial flying then that brought out the braggadocio in people.

"I can remember that night when we had to land at O'Hare on instruments. You couldn't see anything out the window — not even the lights on the tips of the wings." There was a lot of talk like that.

It was important to pick up airline lingo. Saying "Frisco" instead of "San Fran" marked you as an infrequent traveler. To be included in a conversation between two stewardesses was to be accepted as a real insider. The elite flight crews had a sense of mystery about them.

The savvy traveler was able to talk knowingly about various airport terminals. Same thing with different airlines. Businessmen proudly displayed plaques on their office walls showing how many miles they had traveled with each airline.

Talk between passengers was expansive. Since chances were good you would never see the person in the next seat again, you could get by with almost anything. The Walter Mitty next to you passed himself off as a foreign correspondent or a movie director.

The food was better in those days. It tasted less like the microwaved TV dinners you get on airplanes today. And there was more room. You didn't have to keep your elbows tucked under your ribs the way you do now while eating.

Food service was more gracious. On a dinner flight nowadays, the flight attendants race like crazy to get the food down and pick up the trays before the plane reaches its destination.

The booze was complimentary. This was both good and bad. Some passengers used the liquid courage as a means of coping with fear of flying.

With all the free spirits flowing, passengers did overdo. There were occasional flights on which tipsy patrons were given oxygen so that they were able to leave the plane under their own power.

The cost-crunch ended all that. Complimentary beverages now are the traditional coffee, tea or milk, or maybe a half can of Coke in a plastic glass with a couple of ice cubes.

Airline advertising reflects the new financial reality of flying. The pitch these days is the destination and the convenience. It used to be the airlines made getting there important. The trip itself was the thing.

In the reality of today, airline travel isn't the event it once was. With crowded terminals, crowded planes and crowded skies, it has become an unpleasant experience that must be endured.

September 1, 1981

Berg would have loved the attention

THE OTHER SIDE.

How Alan Berg would have loved all the attention he is getting. He would have reveled in the national radio, television and newspaper coverage that has resulted from his gangland-style murder Monday night.

Alan achieved a degree of notoriety in death he never had in life. That life — his loves, his passions, his excesses — is the stuff of which pop legends are made. And like comedian Lenny Bruce, Alan Berg's legacy as gadfly, catalyst and "the man you love to hate" will be around for a long time.

No, I don't know what Alan Berg was *really* like. I knew about parts of him, but I don't believe even he knew where the real Alan Berg ended and his public persona began. As with so many broadcast performers, that is a large, gray area in their lives.

There is something about broadcasting that attracts people who want to be something they aren't. When the studio red light goes on, Walter Mitty stands aside and lets out the submerged ego.

The guy who is a confident, happy-go-lucky, wise-cracking disc jockey on the air in the daytime may well be a brooding drunk consumed with self-doubt at night. What you see and hear is not always the way those people really are.

I had known Alan since the beginning of his radio career in Denver. I appeared several times as a guest on his radio and television shows and had even filled in for him as talk show host when he was on vacation.

Our private conversations revealed a very sensitive Alan Berg. He had superb taste in classical music and jazz. He knew the graphic arts as well. In speaking of these things, the brashness, the vitriol, the rudeness, the irony, the sarcasm were replaced with a kind of quiet urbanity. Can you believe that?

In a strange way, Alan was really the most down-to-earth of his talk-show host contemporaries. I don't think he really took himself seriously at all, as the others do. He never saw himself as journalist, as advocate, as someone with a cause. He was able to laugh at himself, or at what his friend Peter Boyles called Tuesday morning on his talk show "the caricature he created of himself."

He loved fast cars, pretty women, fancy clothes. He learned to talk easily and openly about his personal problems, his weaknesses. He even found amusement in these. So many talk programs these days have become deadly dull serious.

Alan was a realist about what he did. While at KWBZ, he once told me he knew he could never get "big numbers" (audience rating points) until he could move to KOA.

We'll probably never know to what extent, if any, those rating points contributed to his tragic death. The pressure for higher and higher audience ratings can be irresistible. It can push performers beyond the limits of questionable taste into the world of the bizarre, the absurd. Alan Berg was as comfortable in that world as he was in his other world of logic and compassion.

Perhaps we all saw bits and pieces of ourselves in him; things we liked, things we didn't. Alan Berg was loved and hated.

But he was never ignored.

June 20, 1984

'Lord Ivor' knew the royal truth

HOAX.

He could have danced all night: this elegant, tall, slender man with white hair ... *and still have begged for more. He could have spread his wings, and done a thousand things he'd never done before.*

It was almost a reversal of the "My Fair Lady" plot. But the Eliza Doolittle in this rags-to-riches drama was not a young cockney woman, but a Denver bum. And the Professor Henry Higgins was really our own Frances Melrose, editor of the News magazine section in 1949.

Frances has done interesting historical accounts about so many others. I find it fascinating she hasn't written about Lord Ivor, a yarn in which she and former News photographer Bill Peery were key figures.

Perhaps the deception's genesis goes back to Pygmalion, mythological king of ancient Cyprus who fell in love with a statue of Aphrodite. In Ovid's "Metamorphoses," the statue comes to life. William Gilbert adapted the myth into "Pygmalion and Galatea." Then came George Bernard Shaw with his comedy "Pygmalion," which then evolved into "My Fair Lady."

"We were always looking for feature story ideas," Frances recalled. "Bill suggested we find a skid row bum, clean him up and make him a king for a day. It was Bill's idea, but of course he let me do all the work.

"I called the Salvation Army and explained what I wanted. They found a slender man with white hair, gave him a bath, haircut and shave, and dressed him in some respectable clothing.

"We arranged with Harry Anholt, then manager of the Brown Palace Hotel, to give him the presidental suite for the night. Special stationery was printed with the name 'Lord Ivor' embossed at the top."

The man, whose real name was unknown, told Peery he had been married to a socially ambitious woman. After he left her, he said he wanted to make a lot of money and return someday to embarrass her. "But the bottle got the better of him," Peery said.

"We hired a model as his escort and took him to the Beacon Supper Club, a good place to be seen in those days. He sipped champagne, danced, and we introduced him to everyone as 'Lord Ivor.' No one seemed to notice he didn't have a British accent," Frances said. "We did have to keep prompting him on his table manners though."

Peery remembered taking him to the Denver Country Club. He was immediately accepted as Lord Ivor. "No one questioned his background, even though a few hours earlier, our member of royalty was living in an alley and sleeping in the gutter."

Accompanying Frances' News story were Peery's two pictures of Lord Ivor: one sipping champagne with the model and the other showing him asleep in the doorway of a flop house.

"When we dropped him off at the Brown, Lord Ivor asked me for a dollar," Peery said. "I watched him in my rear view mirror. I don't believe he spent the night at the hotel. I saw him take my dollar and go right into the nearest bar. It was kind of sad."

The name Lord Ivor? "It was just a name that popped into my mind when I started working on the story," Frances said.

September 18, 1983

Night encounter bestirs memories

THE EDGE.

It must have been about 10:30 p.m. when I walked back alone from the Hilton Hotel to the parking lot behind the Rocky Mountain News. I had attended the Colorado Sports Hall of Fame banquet.

Only a few cars remained in the lot. My little Volkswagen was somewhere near the center. I was just fishing my keys from my pocket when I spotted something that looked like a little ball of fur.

In the dim light it looked for all the world like a cat. It was sort of hunched up as though it were trying to keep warm in the cold night.

I walked closer, thinking maybe it had been hurt. But just as I was reaching down to touch it, it hopped a few feet away. Yes, hopped away. It was a rabbit. Lordy!

Did you ever see a rabbit downtown? I did. There it was, hunched up again, looking at me with those big brown eyes. That was when I started rubbing my eyes. I looked again, the bunny was still there.

I know what you are thinking and you are wrong. I was stone cold sober. I have seen rabbits before and that was clearly a rabbit — long ears, puff of a tail, the whole shot.

I looked around to see if anyone else was near. Not a soul. Just the old geezer and the rabbit. That's when I began to feel I wasn't alone anymore. I have always thought I was able to sense the presence of those who have departed this level of existence.

I closed my eyes again and saw Lee Casey, columnist and associate editor of the Rocky for many years. After his death Jan. 29, 1951, he was cremated. His ashes were placed in the wall of the News building, right across the street from where I stood.

Then I felt Mary Coyle Chase was near. She was a former News reporter who won the Pulitzer Prize for her play "Harvey," the story of tipsy Elwood P. Dowd and his best friend, a wise and invisible rabbit 6 feet 1½ inches tall. She died Oct. 20, 1981.

I knew and loved them both. Mary always denied it, but many still believe Elwood P. Dowd, was in part modeled after Casey. Having seen "Harvey" on both stage and screen, I certainly saw similarities.

I was always in awe of Casey. His columns were masterpieces, the last of which was an observation that mankind is still faced with the "Irreconcilable Conflict" as it was when the Spartans fought the Athenians in the Peloponnesian War. He was such a fragile, courtly, intelligent little man.

I would occasionally have "lunch" at 5 p.m. with Casey, Pat Patterson and Charlotte Blackman at Shaner's on 17th Street. Pat, Charlotte and I would have sandwiches. Casey would order a beer and a double shot of bourbon.

The parking lot wasn't empty anymore. It was getting crowded. The rabbit and I were in the company of old friends. The night wasn't cold by then. It was warmed by memories and by almost-forgotten feelings.

The rabbit turned and hopped away toward Colfax and Copperfields, where the old White Mule bar used to be. I don't know whether I'll ever see him again, but if I do, I'm going to call him Harvey. And if he starts to get bigger and begins to talk . . .

Am I getting too close to the edge?

March 18, 1984

The granddaddy of all columnists

THIRSTY.

Having lost my grasp on elementary school tradition in this town, I don't know whether kindergartners are still taken on the obligatory tour of the Eugene Field House at the edge of Washington Park.

I can still remember the hushed silence more than 50 years ago when our little class tip-toed through the former Denver home of the man who wrote "The Sugar Plum Tree," "Little Boy Blue" and other selections.

Field's house had been moved to 715 S. Franklin St. from its original location next to the U.S. Mint on West Colfax. None other than "Unsinkable" Molly Brown paid for the move.

I had never heard of Molly Brown when I was a squirt, but I knew all about how "Wynken, Blynken and Nod one night sailed off in a wooden shoe; Sailed on a river of misty light into a sea of dew." It was Field's best-known poem.

I also didn't realize it then, but I was in the home of the granddaddy of all newspaper columnists. Field was hired by the Denver Tribune in 1879 for $35 a week to begin what we now call personal commentary.

Tribune staffers were not fond of Field because of his high salary and because he frequently drank himself into a stupor, missing deadlines.

Even so, Field became a sensation. He invented most of his stuff. He once revealed what he claimed were innermost secrets of 12 of Brigham Young's widows. Actually, he never talked to any of them.

In another column, Field quoted Horace Tabor as saying, "What did he ever do for Colorado?" when Tabor saw a picture of William Shakespeare in the opera house he had just built on Curtis Street. The silver baron was enraged and wanted to go after Field with a gun.

Things became so hot that Field finally had to leave town. He departed on the first Burlington Denver-to-Chicago passenger train in 1881. The rear car was loaded with free booze and food for newspaper reporters.

His friends locked up Field in a "stag" hotel room in Chicago until he became sober enough to seek work. But he bribed a bellboy, got drunk all over again and left.

When his pals got back to the empty room they found a poem on the bedside table. They took it to Melville Stone, editor of the Chicago Evening News. It was on the basis of that poem that Field was hired and became famous for his "Sharps and Flats" column.

The line in the poem that impressed Stone was "The clink of the ice in the pitcher as the boy comes down the hall."

The editor said later that no one could have written those words who had not experienced a morning-after thirst. "I want men who write from the heart, not the head," Stone said.

Field then quit drinking and turned out the best columns of his career. Most of the things he wrote about early Denver and Leadville were really written in Chicago. He loved Denver and wanted to return, but he was afraid of the consequences of some of his columns.

August 23, 1983

Max was a marvel in any challenge

TURMOIL.

"I'm through with you unless you start looking like a human being. You're drab, dull, old, a bum. I've bought a nice new outfit for you at the Denver Dry, and I'll thank you to pick it up on your way to the office."

Elsie Greedy said that 33 years ago to her husband, Max, then news editor of the Rocky Mountain News. When Max picked up his new wardrobe, he was astonished to find a flashy cowboy outfit with bright green shirt, form-fitting trousers, high-heeled boots and 10-gallon hat.

Until then, Max had regarded clothing as simply protection against the elements. The seat of his shapeless pants was shiny. His sleeves were rolled to the elbow. He looked like what he was; a sometimes-gruff, always-demanding, tough news editor.

Max showed up the next day looking like Hoot Gibson. The cowboy hat had replaced the green eye shade. Some said Max had even learned to roll Bull Durham cigarettes with one hand.

As the Rocky Mountain News enters its 126th year, I thought about Max and the colorful people like him who have been involved with the real guts of this newspaper. He retired in 1973 after working here for half a century. He died July 25, 1978.

There was virtually no newsroom job Max didn't perform over those 50 years. But he was essentially an editor. He loved the challenge of tearing up Page One and starting over when a late story broke.

Dec. 7, 1941, Max got out an "extra" edition on the attack on Pearl Harbor in record time. Not satisfied with that, he grabbed 200 copies of the News and ran out and sold them on 17th Street.

Max was a superb editor. He believed there is no such thing as copy that can't be edited, including the Bible and the complete works of Shakespeare.

As headline writer, Max had no peer. When Dr. Barbara Moore, the British vegetarian, walked across the United States in 1960, she came through Denver. The News had followed every step, even sending reporter Leo Zuckerman to accompany her to Denver from Utah. At one point, Leo telephoned the city desk: "You better bring me in. She's beginning to look good to me."

The day Moore arrived, News readers saw on Page One: "**SHE'S HERE!**" It was as though there had been a Second Coming and the savior was a woman.

Another Greedy classic turned up during the Cold War. After an inconclusive debate before the United Nations General Assembly, News readers were reassured by the Page One headline: "**NO WAR.**"

My favorite Greedy headline was written just before deadline one evening when no major story dominated the news. There were the usual problems with the economy, strife in the Middle East, Central American revolutions, border fighting in Asia, labor unrest in Europe, etc.

Max stewed right up to the last minute, unable to make up his mind over which story to use for his Page One headline. Finally, just as time ran out, he tapped out the headline: "**WORLD IN TURMOIL!**"

Hey Max, wherever you are, it still is.

April 22, 1984

Social circles

PEOPLE DON'T SEEM TO HAVE FUN ANYMORE.

Even comedians take themselves too seriously. So do politicians, environmentalists, bureaucrats and a lot of other people. If youth has a common denominator these days, it would certainly have to be grimness.

It wasn't that way with Jack Mohler.

When he died Monday, he left us with memories of the good times — the fun times. The very best of them were right here at the Rocky Mountain News where Mohler was a crime reporter, a feature writer and a society editor.

Society editor?

Yes. There was no small amount of mischief in editor Jack Foster's heart when he named Mohler society editor in 1952. Mohler always claimed the appointment had helped him kill Denver society. That's not entirely true. Kill it, he didn't. Change it, he certainly did.

Horseplay was his stock in trade. With Mohler, the practical joke was much more than a skill. It was an art form. Once, he hired a Chinese midget to stand in Dan Cronin's locker. When the unsuspecting Cronin opened the door, the midget sprayed him with a bottle of seltzer water.

When Foster named Mohler society editor, it was sort of like putting a frog in the punch bowl. Mohler was offended that few Jews could set foot in the Denver Country Club. Because of this, he set about covering social events that took place at Wade's Keg Buffet, the Denver Press Club, the Beacon Supper Club and Jimmy DeCredico's Dome Tavern.

New names began to appear in the society column. There was Bernie the Mudlark and Warren St. Thomas, owner of the infamous Tropics nightclub. Ova Elijah "Smiling Charlie" Stevens also was in there. He was what we used to call "a known gambling figure." Other "socialites" Mohler liked to plug included Jack Albi, Jack Shaner and Jerry Bakke.

Some of the so-called 400 didn't take kindly to all of this social integration. Continental Air Lines' Bob Six wanted Mohler's hide. So did a good many of Denver's social-climbing nouveaux riches. Mohler was surprised and delighted to learn, however, that Mrs. Claude Boettcher, Mrs. Spencer Penrose, Mrs. Joe Fisher, Mrs. A.E. Carlton and Mrs. Henry Van Schaack never missed his column and loved every line of it. Mohler called them his "Real Society."

The readership of Mohler's column increased rapidly. It even surpassed "Molly Mayfield," the popular lovelorn column written by Foster's wife, Frankie. This created no little tension around the News since Mrs. Foster was something of a socialite herself.

Mohler finally let all of the air out of Denver society when he covered a farewell cocktail party of a black elevator operator at the

Statehouse. About the incident, he wrote in The Denver Magazine, "Jeesus Keeryst, you would have thought I had set fire to the Denver Athletic Club."

In 1954, Mohler took to the airwaves with his own radio program. It was called "Talk of the Town" and it was on KMYR. It was a late-night show that originated from Eddy Ott's "Sherman Plaza." Mohler had a corner booth where he chatted more with waitresses than he did with Junior Leaguers.

On one memorable program, a prominent society figure in the next booth slumped over dead. Mohler hardly glanced up. He just bantered away through the rest of the program as though nothing had happened.

He was a fine writer. Mohler practiced his craft among some of the best. His special friends then, and at the time of his death, were Sam Lusky and Pasquale Marranzino.

Jack Mohler was certainly irreverent when it came to the "400." Among them, he said, ". . . were stuffed shirts, check kiters, cheaters at gin, besotted souls and minds, mountebanks and thieves." Also, there were ". . . some of the finest, decentest and most exciting folks in Colorado."

Jack, you were one of the really decent ones, yourself. We'll miss you. We all loved you very much.

April 27, 1978

On Irish whiskey and a joyful soul

Cuz.

The tiny Mother of God Church at Speer Boulevard and Logan Street was filled with people trying to pray Leonard Tangney into heaven. And when the last Hail Marys were said, a tenor sang "On Galway Bay."

Leonard was not one of your "two-sprinkle" Catholics. There was more to his faith than getting doused with holy water at baptism and death. Mother Church was important to him, and it was one of the few institutions in life he wouldn't kid about.

And so it was appropriate that there were at least seven priests in white vestments involved in the rosary and memorial Mass. It was a celebration of the new life we all prayed Leonard would have.

As I listened to the priest intoning the Five Joyful Mysteries, I looked around at the faces. There were old Irish faces, old Catholic faces, old editors' faces, old reporters' faces, old authors' faces. And there were pretty, young faces, too. Leonard would have liked that.

Of the more than 46 years Leonard worked as a newspaperman, 35 of them were at the Rocky Mountain News as a copy editor, editor for features and assistant news editor. Our people were at the funeral, of course, but so were many of his friends from the Denver Post and old pals from the Denver Press Club.

If Leonard's spiritual home was the Catholic Church, his social home was certainly the Press Club. He had been its president in 1959 and 1960 and had served on the board of directors for seven terms. When he was sitting at the bar, he was always good for an Irish Mist or two.

I suspect people like Leonard are the reason so many of us stay in this game. He was irrepressible, jaunty, full of blarney, and more than anything else, he was Leonard.

There was a time — about 25 years ago — that Leonard and I looked alike. Same color hair, same deep lines in the face, same nose, same glasses. And as luck would have it, we lived in the same neighborhood and shopped at the same little drug store on East Sixth Avenue.

One day he stopped by the store and picked up some razor blades, a bottle of Old Bushmills Irish whiskey and a carton of cigarettes. As the young woman behind the counter was making out the ticket, she said, "Shall I charge these, Mr. Amole?"

I can almost see Leonard's face as she got to the Mr. Amole part. I don't imagine his expression changed at all, but there must have been a brief impish look flash in his eyes as he said offhandedly, "Yes, why don't you do that."

He couldn't wait until the end of the month when I got the bill. He confessed what he had done, and because of our resemblance, he declared us, "cousins." That's how I became his "cuz."

When the Mass was over, the Rev. Charles B. Woodrich walked down the aisle and stopped where I was sitting. He pointed at me and said, "We're next."

I don't know whether that is true, nor do I know if we managed to pray Leonard into heaven. But when my time comes, I hope I can go wherever he is. That's where the fun will be.

Later, Cuz.

October 4, 1984

Red respected simple courtesy

RED.

Remember 30 years ago when Sen. Joe McCarthy was terrorizing the nation? "I'd rather be dead than Red," he would shout.

Red Fenwick, in that impudent, puckish way of his would respond, "All things considered, I think I would rather be Red than dead." Well, Red is dead. He suffered a heart attack Thursday at Cheyenne. He will be buried there Monday.

Old Red lived every minute of his 73 years. He might have been able to hang in there a little longer if he had taken it a little easier on the corners during his salad days. But I can almost hear him saying, "This old jasper wouldn't change a minute of it."

Even though Red lived in Denver many years, I'm not surprised he is being buried in Wyoming. Writing in his Denver Post column years ago, Red made it clear where his loyalties were:

"Ask most any old-timer up in Wyoming what he thinks about the state and chances are he'll haul off and cuss up a purple storm. But suggest that he move elsewhere and you've a fight on your hands. To the ground-tied, raised-in-the-rough Wyomingite, there simply isn't any other place fit for human habitation unless, maybe, it's Colorado or Montana, and there is some doubt about these two."

Reared in the rough he was. Red was born in Indiana, spent his early childhood in Kentucky and lived much of his boyhood in Wyoming.

"Douglas is my old hometown," he used to say.

It has been written elsewhere how Red worked as a telephone lineman and a cowboy, and how he served a hitch in the horse cavalry. He was largely self-educated. Even though he knew how to write "proper English," as he called it, Red's columns echoed with Western voices.

I always thought I could "hear" Red's quotes. He had that knack of being able to lift a sentence from a page and give it sound. His dialects were never forced. They were natural, authentic. He and Will Rogers were the only two men I ever heard who could use the word "folks" without making it sound condescending.

Red's affection for the rural West was genuine. Right before the National Western Stock Show each year, he'd write a predictable column about how open, honest and trustworthy Westerners are. I talked to him about this once. He convinced me he really believed it. That conviction came through in his columns. In the many rough characters who lived in his writing, there was a fundamental decency to all of them.

His columns made the West seem like everyone's back yard. He wanted us all to feel like neighbors.

"A fellow who doesn't push somebody will stay a long time at the hindmost nipple where the milk is lean and less," he wrote.

"He is ridiculed, scorned, passed up, stepped on, knocked around and overlooked, but he's polite, he believes in his country and his fellow man. But what is more important, there are 75 million others just like him."

Yup.

November 7, 1982

'Old warhorse' goes to pasture in style

KING JACK.

It wasn't until after he died two years ago at 82 that I learned Jack Fitzpatrick's real name was Jacques LeRoi Fitzpatrick. Translated from French, I guess that means "Jack the King." To me, he was just Uncle Jake.

Others called him Fitz. Many of his pals who worked at his side covering Statehouse news referred to him as *El Pedo Viejo*, an affectionate Spanish idiom I am not about to translate for you.

Jack has been designated posthumously by the Denver Press Club as Colorado Communicator of the Year. A bronze plaque honoring him will be dedicated Wednesday at the Daniels and Associates Communications Center, 2930 E. Third Ave.

His name will be placed next to those of Thomas Hornsby Ferril, Gene Cervi, Hugh Terry, Palmer Hoyt, Gene O'Fallon, Jack Foster and others who have distinguished themselves in the media crafts.

I can't recall how many retirement parties I attended for Jack. He loved them all, beaming as one speaker after another rose to highlight the glossier chapters in his long newspaper and broadcasting careers.

The best of those parties was in 1970 when he retired from KHOW.

At 70, everyone said he had earned retirement and a chance to spend more time with his lovely wife, Leona, who is still living. A statement to me at that dinner by the late Dan Thornton, former Colorado governor, proved prophetic. "I refuse to believe the old warhorse will finally go out to pasture," he said.

Instead of going out to pasture, Jack came to work the next morning as though the party the night before had never occurred. He worked every day until he was 80, finally forced to quit because of heart, lung, kidney and vision problems.

Of the countless stories Jack and I covered together, the dynamiting Feb. 25, 1950, of the giant 350-foot Grant Smelter smokestack lives most vividly in my memory. Jack represented KFEL. The late Mack Switzer was there for KLZ, Starr Yelland was broadcasting for KOA and I was KMYR's reporter.

Hundreds of thousands of people turned out to watch the condemned historic stack destroyed. I was doing the only live broadcast when the explosion finally went off, five hours after it had been scheduled. The other stations had gone on to network programming, Jack was recording the event on an old Webcor wire recorder.

When the massive pink cloud of brick dust rolled over everything, I saw Jack wheezing and swearing as he tried to protect his recorder from the dust. The recording was ruined. Jack told me later, "That was the greatest story I never covered."

Uncle Jake seemed a cantankerous curmudgeon. But as Tom Gavin wrote, he was really "a fraud," pretending to be the cynic everyone expects reporters to be, but he was really a "compassionate softy."

And as Fred Brown noted in his eulogy, "He loved to be where the action was, whether the game was politics or baseball. He lived and died as most of us can only hope to — with grace and wit and love until a quick and peaceful end."

July 24, 1984

Now that he's lost, it's 'good old Bill'

AN ERA.

When you get to be my age, life becomes one era after another. Just as one ends, there's another waiting in the wings. The latest to end is the William H. McNichols Jr. era at City Hall. You can tell his era has ended because people are saying such nice things about him.

No one had a good word for Bill McNichols until he was defeated in Tuesday's election. But now, his enemies are showering him with compliments.

"Good old Bill," they say with misty-eyed fondness. "The old boy had his faults, but he really knew how to run a city. We were lucky to have him. This town had unprecedented growth under Mayor Bill."

Generating that kind of warmth are usually the ones who are trying to grab his support for the runoff. But having been around the track many times, he probably knows this.

The end of the McNichols era reminds me somewhat of the end of the Ben Stapleton era 35 years ago. It ended when both daily newspapers came out against him. It is tough to survive that kind of editorial opposition.

Stapleton was elected mayor in 1923, the year I was born. His era lasted until 1947. The only break came in 1931 when he lost a single term to George Begole, the mayor no one remembers.

I grew to manhood thinking Ben Stapleton had permanent possession of City Hall in much the same way the pope was chosen to run the Roman Catholic Church for life.

I was a young reporter when his era ended. It wasn't really my story. I sort of nibbled at its edges. But the times were exciting. I liked the idea of the old machine being thrown out and new people coming in.

The reformer who replaced Stapleton was Quigg Newton, an aristocratic young lawyer. He enjoyed unprecedented support of both newspapers and both political parties. Former reporters Gene Cervi and Ralph Radetsky masterminded his campaign.

It was obvious early on election night that Newton had won a smashing victory. There was a lot of talk of how an era was ending and how old Ben Stapleton hadn't really been so bad after all.

He gave us our airport, and his manager of parks and improvements, elegant old George Cranmer, had built the amphitheater at Red Rocks and our mountain parks system. Good old Ben. Good old George.

The Newton era lasted eight years. Then we had shorter eras named after Mayors Will Nicholson, Richard Batterton and Thomas Currigan. The length of an era is precisely the same as the popularity duration of the man after whom it is named

I don't have a handle yet on the next era. The News and the Post don't agree on this generation's reform candidate. The News is supporting Federico Peña and the Post is for Dale Tooley. That makes the runoff campaign more interesting.

But down the road, when the rascal is finally turned out, people will look down in their drinks election night and will remember that good old Dale, or good old Federico, was not such a bad mayor after all.

May 19, 1983

Memories crowd out the loneliness

LONELY.

I was waiting in the drive-through line at a Wendy's in Fort Collins when I heard on the radio that Ethel Merman had died. The newscaster said her favorite role was Mama Rose in the Broadway musical, "Gypsy."

My mind went back 30 years when her favorite real-life role in Denver was also Mama. It was after she married Bob Six, then president of Continental Airlines.

Denver has always cherished its resident celebrities, and so it seemed to follow that she would be welcomed with open arms. But it didn't work out quite that way.

Six had purchased a home in Cherry Hills Village. That's when the ugly whispers began. Some of the suburb's glossier residents weren't quite sure they wanted a Jew in their neighborhood. It didn't seem to matter that no one was really certain she was Jewish. Six persisted and they moved in without incident.

At the same time, I was living in an $11,000 Hutchinson-Carey house in nearby University Hills. We used to joke that you could go from rags to riches simply by crossing East Hampden Avenue.

Much to everyone's surprise, Ethel enrolled her 10-year-old daughter in the choir at Christ Episcopal Church and Mama was there every Sunday morning to watch and to be proud. During those hymns in which the congregation also sang, there was no mistaking Ethel's raspy voice rising above the others.

During that same period, I was assigned to interview her. I can remember how nervous I was as I was shown into her home. At one end of the huge living room was a life-size oil painting of Ethel dressed in the costume of Panama Hattie.

When I admired the painting, she offered to show me her art collection after we had finished the interview. I could tell she didn't recognize me from church.

After I closed my tape recorder, we toured every room in the house. It was filled with lovely French impressionist oils, so unlike what I would have imagined her tastes to be. I guess I was misled by her brassy persona on stage.

"My favorite painting is this Raoul Dufy," she said, only she pronounced it DUF-ee, as though it were Duffy instead of doo-FEE. "I also like his brother, Jack," I knew she must have been referring to Dufy's lesser known brother, Jacques.

Oh, I didn't laugh. I realized she was very serious. She might not have known how to pronounce French properly, but she certainly knew art. We talked a long time. I felt then that she was a very lonely woman. There didn't seem to be anyone in our town with whom she could identify. I have since thought maybe we didn't try hard enough to know her for what she was, not just what she seemed to be.

But my memory is not all sad. I can still see her as Mama, standing proudly in the back row of that little church as her daughter sang with the choir. She seemed happy in that off-stage role.

Quote: *The sound of applause is delicious.* — a line from Gypsy.

February 16, 1984

A taste of that old ethnic flavor

YICHUS.

Sometime between then and now, Denver lost the ethnic flavor of its old neighborhoods. By homogenizing races, national origins and creeds, we changed the city's texture, and not necessarily for the better.

There is a Yiddish word that describes the sense of community in those old neighborhoods. It is *yichus,* a special closeness, almost a sense of family.

The Jewish community bounded by Federal Boulevard, Meade Street, West 13th Avenue and Conejos Place had *yichus.* Its immigrants had lived under the West Colfax viaduct. As times got better, they moved "up the hill."

I know because I was a *shaygets,* or gentile boy, who grew up on Newton Street. That's where I knew Ben Reiff, Leonard "Chink"

Alterman and Leon Goldfogel. We all went to Lake Junior High, where Anna Laura Force was the principal and the law. It was also where I had very secret crushes on Shana Goldberg and Cecille Lande.

Leon, Chink and Ben were all members of the Arrow Club, which started in 1934 at the Guldman Community Center. Its theme was "Learn to be leaders." Arrow boys memorized such homilies as, "It's a wise boy who knows he isn't."

Some of the other Arrow boys were: Nate Blumberg, now professor of journalism at the University of Montana; Harold "Puppy" Friedland; Vic Seidenberg, an old pal of mine when he and his brother, Max, ran the Assembly Bar and Grill; Sidney "Smokey" Milzer; and Sam "Sugie" Sugarman.

The Arrows are celebrating their 50th anniversary Aug. 2 at the Holiday Inn on Chambers Road. Joining them will be about 150 other *menshen* who grew up in the same neighborhood. The list is too long for this column, but in it are movers and shakers who have contributed significantly to this old town.

All the Perlmutters will be there, Ben, Jordy, Jack, Joe and Leonard. What they haven't built, Sam Primack has. He'll be there, too. So will U.S. District Judge Sherman "Sherm-the-Firm" Finesilver.

Former Colorado Supreme Court Chief Justice Edward Pringle is invited. So is "Papa" Joe Luby and City Auditor Mike Licht. Leo "Blindy" Zuckerman, a former ink stain here at the Rocky and now a lawyer, is a West Side boy. So is Irv Brown, coach/referee/TV-radio commentator. You couldn't keep Joe "Awful" Coffee away.

Rabbis Daniel Goldberger and Manuel "Manny" Laderman still live in the neighborhood near the Hebrew Educational Alliance. But almost all the rest have moved out. They are living in places such as Cherry Hills Village, Hilltop, Crestmoor and Greenwood Village. Not bad for a bunch of kids, many of whom were born of parents who lived under the viaduct and couldn't speak English.

The old neighborhood is gone, but the *yichus* remains. Ben Reiff was kind enough to invite me, but I'll be out of town. I would have enjoyed the good company. It was my dear friend Ben Bezoff who once said to me, "Geneula, you are almost Jewish. Almost, but not quite."

Mazel tov!

July 29, 1984

New 17th Street as good as ever

Where were you the day the Old Nostalgia burned down? I was standing in front of Clark's Drug Store at the corner of 17th and Stout streets, just across from the stately old Equitable Building.

I went back to that same spot the other day just to remember. Thank heavens the Equitable is still there. It reminds us of the way 17th Street used to be, and the way we were. The lobby is still cool and serene with its vaulted mosaic ceilings, stunning stained glass windows, gleaming brass and its polished green and wine-colored tile.

But Clark's and its thick milkshakes are gone, as is the Albany and Danny's Shine Parlor. All have been replaced by a monolith called the Petro-Lewis Building. Of the old enterprises, I suppose I miss Danny's the most.

Danny Abeyta, "Mayor of 17th Street," as News columnist Pocky Marranzino called him, came from Trinidad (ours, not the island). Like many from this old coal mining town, Danny knew how to work, how to hustle, how to make something of his life.

The width of Danny's Shine Parlor was no more than eight feet. But he somehow managed to squeeze six shine chairs into it, plus a hat-cleaning-and-blocking business in the back.

At first, a shine was 15 cents, later 25. Danny paid the shine boys $3 a day and all the tips they could earn. As the flannel cloths snapped and popped across wing-tipped shoes, Danny's clientele talked mostly of football, horse racing, the stock market and other ventures of chance.

A block or so away, Saliman's became noted for, of all things, its breaded veal cutlets and country gravy. If you wanted hot kosher corned beef sliced paper thin and stacked high between thick slices of pumpernickel, you went to Shaner's.

Timmy Shaner stirred a very arid and very crisp martini, or "Mother Shaner's deep-dish olive pie," as some called it. Guitarist Johnny Smith stopped by evenings to play "Moonlight in Vermont." I don't remember the name of the kid with a crew cut who blew flugelhorn.

There was Elmer's Barber Shop, Pohndorf's Jewelry, the formidable brownstone Denver Club, Jacobson's tobacco shop, the Algerian and Club 400. And over on 16th Street, convention delegates bellied up to the bar at the Yacht Club, later Chez Paree.

I loved the old 17th Street, but I like the new one, too. I miss Johnny Megill, bartender at the Albany, but now it's fun to watch slick businessladies prance up the street.

Sure, I wish Lou Coffee's Steak House was still there, but now I have the street vendors who sell everything from hot dogs to fruit and nuts to flowers.

Jazz? The new 17th Street has its sound, too. I saw a black man in a wheelchair on Glenarm Place. His red baseball cap was on backward and he was improvising both the chorus and verse of "Stardust."

It was a lovely, wistful sound in such a busy place. As I walked from the past into the present, I could hear the lyrics in my mind:
Sometimes I wonder why I spend these lonely hours . . .
May 20, 1984

A time traveler on Tremont Place

WHITE PLUME.

It's a shame H.G. Wells didn't build his time machine on Tremont Place where 18th Avenue intersects Broadway. It would have been a great vantage point to sample some dramatic moments in Denver history.

At the urging of News feature writers Marge Barrett and Irene Clurman, I walked up Tremont from West Colfax Avenue to visit the new Museum of Western Art in the old Navarre Building. I rejoice that our downtown streets are slanty. That's such a nice view of the old stone spire of Trinity Methodist Church as you walk northeast on Tremont.

The interesection is in transition. Workers are gutting the old Cosmopolitan Hotel. As I looked at those glassless windows, my mental time machine switched on. I saw the old Broadway Theater at the south end of the hotel. And then an ugly day in 1940 rushed into sharp focus. A man jumped from a sixth-floor window of the Cosmo and splattered on the glass and steel canopy over the 18th Avenue entrance.

A bellboy ran out the door, looked up at the rag-doll body and then at the open window. He returned to the lobby, took the elevator to the sixth floor, found the room and opened the door. It was a collage of glasses, cigarette butts, empty bottles and dirty clothes. By the open window was an unsigned note: "If you don't think this takes guts, try it yourself."

I was the bellboy.

The only way to find Boggio's Rotisserie now is in a time machine. Look at the infinite variety of pasta on the menu. The world's best minestrone, bread sticks, wine sundaes — all lost in time.

If time seems to slip away more quickly than is your taste, be refreshed at your first view of the beautifully restored Navarre, 1727 Tremont Place. There it is, where it has been since 1880.

No longer a girls' school/gambling hall/brothel/restaurant/jazz joint/residence, all of which it has been, the Navarre is now a superb Museum of Western Art. It wears its new identity well. And a $3 tour from the third floor down to the basement is a journey in a different sort of time machine.

Masterworks by Bierstadt, Moran, Farny, Russell, Remington, Blumenschein, O'Keeffe, Rockwell, Pollack and others will take you to the West "Before the White Man" to "Westward Expansion" and finally to "The Old West is Dead."

The building was named by Ed Chase, who operated it as a gambling hall with Vaso Chucovich. It is believed that Chase named it after white-plumed Henry of Navarre because of his reputation for loving the good life.

In private antique collections around Denver there may still be a few pieces of Navarre china bearing the authentic arms of the tiny kingdom along with white plume that marked Henry at Ivry.

Only the white tile floor in the basement remains. That's where small ivory balls danced on roulette wheels in Chase's time.

Quote: *Time goes, you say? Ah no!/Alas, time stays, we go.* — Austin Dobson.

January 17, 1984

Time to be serious about comedian

THE COMEDIAN.

I suppose it is natural actors want to be singers, singers want to be comedians and comedians want to be taken seriously. Fred Taylor was a very funny man who wanted to be taken seriously.

I don't remember exactly when and where I met Fred and his wife, Fae. It must have been on a club date back in the early 1950s. They had just come from New York to appear in Denver supper clubs after working the legendary Palace Theater and "The Ed Sullivan Show."

They were one of the first record pantomime acts. No one ever did it better. Anyone who saw Fred's pantomime of "Be My Love" was never able to take Mario Lanza's singing seriously again.

Fred was wildly funny on his own. Impossible to top. I can remember what an exhausting experience it was to try to swap gags with him. About the time I thought I had him in a corner, Fred would reach back in his fertile imagination and end the competition with a real zinger.

But he had a problem. It was his voice. He talked in a falsetto because of a malformed larynx. That's probably why he and Fae developed their pantomime act. Given any other kind of voice, Fred would have been a major comedy talent. He had a fine, mobile face and an incredible sense of timing.

Everyone thought Fred and Fae lived exciting, glamorous lives. But one-nighters, club dates, living on the wrong side of the clock, always being on the road — those things can get awfully old. When television came to Denver in 1952, they saw it as a way to get off the treadmill.

Their "Soda Shop" show on Channel 2 was a great success with teen-agers. A strange thing happened. Fred's falsetto became his trademark. It became a fad for high school boys to try to talk in Fred's squeaky voice.

While the show was a success with kids, it wasn't with sponsors. Depressed and frustrated, Fred asked my advice. I told him the only people who like teen-agers are other teen-agers. I suggested he and Fae develop a show for little kids. I don't know whether it was a result of my advice or not, but they did just that and remained at the top of Denver TV on Channels 9 and 7 for a decade.

They stopped doing club dates, raised a family and lived reasonably normal lives in a lovely Lakewood home. Those were their best years, and I remained a close friend during most of that time.

When David Freed wrote that excellent piece last month in the Rocky about children's television a generation ago, I chatted briefly on the telephone with Fae. She has been confined to a wheelchair, as a result of a stroke, since 1974. It was then she told me Fred was hospitalized in Texas.

He died of heart failure Saturday. I have no idea what his last thoughts were. I wish somehow he could have known the things he and Fae did on stage and on TV are fondly remembered by a lot of people.

August 17, 1982

Another lost art

DEPARTMENT STORES.

They are not what they used to be. The merchandise is inferior and so is customer service. Chalk it up to the declining quality of life.

The human element has gone out of merchandising. Nobody knows anything about salesmanship anymore. It is becoming a lost art.

Try to get a little help and the clerk just points to a counter. On it are stacks of identical polyester sports shirts that probably were made in Taiwan.

Even when you do find what you want, you can't find anyone who will take your money. There usually is one cashier for every three departments. He or she is besieged with customers who are irritable because they have to wait.

No one trusts anyone anymore. Try to write a check for your purchase and the cashier has to telephone someone to see if you have any money in your account.

The system is by no means foolproof. Sometimes the little voice on the other end of the line says your check is no good. The poor clerk has to tell you she can't accept it.

You say that there is plenty of money in your account, and there must be some mistake. The other customers try to act like they don't hear what is happening.

Finally, you get on the phone and it turns out that there has been a computer foul-up and your account number is similar to one that has a poor credit rating.

You have been humiliated, the other customers have been delayed, the clerk is embarrassed and all you get for your money is a lousy polyester sport shirt that probably won't fit.

As you stomp out of the store in a purple rage, it occurs to you that no one even said he was sorry.

This admittedly is a general indictment of department stores. There are exceptions. Some seem to make a sincere effort to offer quality merchandise and good service.

The clerks shouldn't be blamed. They are the victims of the system. In many cases, sales commissions have been taken away and there is little motivation for being of service to the customer.

The decline of the department store began about 15 years ago when the big discount stores moved into the city. There were predictions that the old-fashioned department stores either would be forced out of business or would have to meet cut-rate competition.

As it has turned out, Go-Lo, GEM, Spartan's, Arlan's and the rest have gone belly up. The department stores apparently won. But did they?

The names of the stores are the same, but it seems to the customer that what we are left with is the trashy merchandise and the indifferent service of the discounters.

It used to be a pleasure to shop downtown. Remember? There were little candy and pastry counters. The smell of perfume was in the air. The women in the cosmetic department dressed in black and had pretty hair styles.

The clerks had pride in themselves and in the company they represented. They knew the inventory and would knock themselves out to try to help you.

The merchandise was infinitely better. You knew and trusted the brand names. If something wasn't right, exchanges were made quickly and cheerfully. Department store management was responsive to both employee and customer needs. No one was any better at this than Dave Touff. He used to run May D&F. Touff had good people under him. Lum Jenkins and Jerry Nemiro were a couple of them.

Over at The Denver, Frank Johns always seemed a little stuffy, but he knew how to run a business and the customers responded. What has happened to people like them?

They are gone. What a shame.

October 2, 1979

Farewell, Johnny, my jazzman friend

MUSIC MAN.

Johnny Roberts always took his trombone with him when he traveled. He didn't want to miss any opportunity to sit in with a jazz band, whether it was on a Mississippi riverboat or a basement dive in South Chicago.

I don't know, but I would imagine that when John Taggart Roberts died last week in California, the old tailgate slushpump wasn't far from his side. I heard about his death last week when I was in Dallas covering the Republican National Convention. Knowing of my long friendship with Johnny, someone called the city desk here at the News and asked that I be told.

You know how it is when you hear of the death of someone important to you. You get a mental image of the way you always want to remember that friend. When I closed my eyes, I could see Johnny standing there in his tuxedo, holding his trombone, a big grin on his face, ready to play.

And he could play. Gutty! Back in the late 1930s — that was when he was band instructor in room 565 at South High School — Tommy Dorsey had heard him play with a local jazz band. Dorsey offered Johnny a job only to be turned down because he wanted to work with young high school musicians.

It wasn't always just jazz, though. From 1931 to 1939, Johnny played trombone and tuba with the Denver Symphony Orchestra. He also played as a staff musician under Milton Shrednik at KOA. And during the 1938-39 season, he was baritone horn soloist with the City Park municipal band.

Johnny retired from the Denver Public Schools in 1973 after serving 21 years as director of music. It was in that role he touched so many lives over the generations as innovator and educator. He was our Professor Harold Hill, only jazz was the legacy Johnny left. Our Music Man took America's only native folk music out of the joints, the saloons and the bawdy houses and put it into the classrooms.

As a founding member and president of the National Association of Jazz Educators, he brought national recognition to the Denver Public Schools music programs. He believed in music. He felt that instrumentalists and singers, as well as those who just listen, should be exposed to all types of music from "rock to Bach," as he explained it.

Jazz was his first love. He jobbed around a lot, even when he was Denver Public Schools music director. He would just show up and start to play. Once, he organized a hard-swinging big-band jazz ensemble made up entirely of Denver music teachers.

I had a letter from Johnny a couple of months ago. He had been in ill health in recent years. In his fragile handwriting, he expressed pride that the Denver Public Schools Citywide Jazz Ensemble had won first place in the prestigious 1984 Downbeat Magazine competition.

Is there music after death? I don't know. But if there is, there is a man in a tuxedo walking up to the bandstand. There is a grin on his face and a trombone in his hands.

He probably will say, "Hey man, mind if I sit in?" And then someone — maybe Bix or Fats — will kick off the tempo, and the band will play "Oh, Didn't He Ramble!"

August 28, 1984

Charles Atlas wouldn't shrug

POSTPAID.

My addiction to sending away for things in the mail goes back to the time I was a 12-year-old boy and had scarlet fever. The doctor had made me stay home in bed for a couple of weeks.

I was a devotee of what we then called dime novels. In the hierarchy of pulp literature, they came along somewhere between penny dreadfuls and comic books. My favorites were "Lone Eagle," "G-8 and His Battle Aces" and "Doc Savage."

I had read almost everything in the house during the first week of recuperation. That's when I began to fill out coupons from the advertisements. The first one I mailed was to Charles Atlas.

By employing his "dynamic tension" discovery, he was going to make me a new man in just seven days. Even though no one had kicked sand in my face at the beach, it seemed like a good idea since I was a 97-pound weakling. I also sent for information from the International Correspondence School and LaSalle University.

I'd watch each day for the mailman and his armload of catalogs. It seemed like a miracle I could get all that attention with just a penny post card. It made me feel like a big deal when the envelope was addressed to "Mr." Gene Amole.

I thought I had outgrown all that until Mark Stevens gave me an L.L. Bean catalog the other day. I'm hooked again. L.L. Bean in Freeport, Maine, is a mail-order company specializing in clothing, camping equipment and other outdoor merchandise.

I went bananas. My order for oxford cloth shirts, dress chino slacks, Baxter State Parka, corduroy jeans, Bean's Norwegian sweater and a pair of corduroy espadrilles for Trish came to $220.

If there had been another line on the order form, I would have sent away for Bean's "superior worsted wool whipcord trousers." They would bring out the forest ranger in me. I like the idea of leather trim on the flapped pockets.

I will order them next time around. I'm also going to get a Hatteras rope hammock, an Icelandic wool jacket, an electric meat smoker, trapper blankets, a pair of lined moosehide slippers and a Schrade lockblade bear-paw knife.

While I'm at it, I am going to send away for a Land's End "direct merchants" catalog. They are overstocked on aneroid ship-strike barometers. I absolutely have to have one. If I hurry, I may be able to pick up one for $150.

Land's End has a snappy-looking Navy pea coat for $72.50. I'll also order a Hurricane Hook boomerang, a Barleycorn tweed jacket, several pairs of traditional Scottish argyle socks, a square-rigger attache case, weather-resistant chukka boots and a pedometer that "accurately registers each step to 25 miles."

I know what you are thinking. You think I'm crazy for sending away for a lot of stuff that is probably available right here in town. That's not the point. It's the magic of having it come through the mail.

You don't suppose Charles Atlas is still in business, do you? Never can tell when some bully will kick sand in your face.

August 22, 1982

Legendary lawyer

ACCIDENTAL SHOOTING.

The jury didn't believe Jean Harris when she testified that her gun accidentally discharged three times, killing Dr. Herman Tarnower, her lover and the author of "The Complete Scarsdale Medical Diet." The incident occurred March 10, a cottage cheese day, at his expensive Purchase, N.Y., estate.

After deliberating eight days, the jury decided Harris gunned down the wealthy physican in a jealous rage over his affair with a younger and more attractive woman. The former headmistress at fashionable Madeira School for girls faces a prison term of 15 years to life.

It's too bad Fred Dickerson wasn't alive to defend her. During his distinguished 53-year Colorado law career, the gravel-voiced attorney was counsel for 68 accused murderers. Most of them were acquitted.

He would have claimed that Harris could not be held accountable for the crime because of a protein deficiency. This would have resulted in an involuntary twiching of her finger, causing the pistol to go off repeatedly. He would have convicted the cottage cheese.

A master courtroom tactician, Dickerson was tall, angular. His face was a leathery brown, and his bald head was fringed with a halo of close-cropped white hair. He blamed his hair loss on the time spent during his youth as a miner in Crested Butte.

Dickerson dressed in conservative tweed suits, but he wore colorful argyle socks. When an unfriendly witness was giving damaging testimony. Dickerson would cross his legs, hike up his trousers so the jury members could see the vivid hosiery. He would waggle his ankle back and forth, mesmerizing them and diverting their attention from the witness.

One of the accused murders Dickerson defended was a bartender by the name of Joe. He was a large, powerfully built man of Italian heritage. Joe was noted for his quiet stoicism. He rarely said anything, even when pouring boilermakers at the downtown Denver bar where he worked.

As he was shaving one morning, Joe's wife began to nag at him about a variety of domestic problems. He listened quietly as he lathered his face and slipped a new blade into his razor. On and on went the nagging. Joe continued to shave in silence. He didn't make enough money, she said. He worked late. Wouldn't pick up his dirty underwear. Didn't take her anywhere nice.

About the time he had shaved half his face, something snapped inside. Joe put down the razor, went to his dresser drawer, took out a German Luger pistol, and then he coolly pumped eight bullets into his wife, killing her instantly. He went back to the bathroom, finished shaving, splashed on some aftershave and called the police.

Dickerson built Joe's defense on the unlikely supposition that the gun had discharged accidentally — eight times. In the process, Dickerson let it be known what a nagging woman Joe's wife was. The poor, hard-working man never knew a quiet moment at home.

Dickerson's summation was a classic performance. Contortionist style, he re-enacted the struggle over the pistol, taking both Joe's and his wife's roles — simultaneously, of course. Finally, it was over, the judge gave his instructions, the case went to the jury.

It returned almost immediately and acquitted Joe. Surprised and pleased, Dickerson waited in the hall for the foreman. "I'm glad you understood how the pistol accidently discharged repeatedly," Dicker-son said.

"Oh, we didn't believe that," the foreman replied.

"What?"

"Naw, we thought she had it coming."

February 26, 1981

Who needs Bigs? We've got Bears

PLAY BALL!

We've managed to dodge the bullet again, old pals. It's going to be another great summer without the big leagues. We can still go out to the ball park, spend $3.50 for a general admission ticket and watch our Bears.

Yes, this is my annual get-out-and-support-the-Denver-Bears column. It is the one spring ritual during which you generously grant me space to write of baseball's sweeping panorama, of the boy in every man, of what I call "the game of life."

I shivered through the Bears' home opener Friday night and the season's second game Saturday at what we once called Bears Stadium. It will always be Bears Stadium to me, not Mile High Stadium the big-time Charlies renamed it when professional football became our state religion. At least we don't call it Bronco Field.

In times of $40 million quarterbacks, $75 million franchises and other megabuck insanities, a ticket to anything for $3.50 is a bargain beyond belief. The lowest Denver Broncos ticket price is $13.50. The Denver Gold has a bottom price of $8. Only the Denver Nuggets price of $3.30 is lower.

My season tickets are in section 109, just behind the Bears dugout. I like to be close to first base action, even though I still feel somewhat guilty not sitting along the third base line. That's where, as a 3-year-old, I was lectured by Grandpa Will Amole on squeeze-bunt strategies.

My little fanny fit perfectly on those narrow green boards that passed for seats in Merchants Park, or the "Old Brickyard," as we called it back in the 1920s. We never missed a game in The Denver Post Tournament of semipro teams.

Grandpa and I would watch the M&O Cigars, Coors (Prohibition era) Malted Milks, the bearded House of Davids, Kansas City Monarchs with Satchel Paige and Cool Papa Bell, Elitch's and other ball clubs of the period. After the major league season ended, the likes of Dizzy and Daffy Dean, Pepper Martin and Frankie Frisch, "the Fordham Flash," would barnstorm through town and play with the local talent.

You are probably right that my devotion to minor league baseball is a thinly-disguised strategy to recapture a boyhood that long ago slipped into memory. Even so, the Bears have so long been a part of our heritage they should be given historic preservation designation.

There'll be a day, I suppose, when some fickle major league owner will turn his back on tradition in another city and move his team here to plunder our nouveau riche treasures. I'll be standing in line with the rest to buy a ticket. But when the inevitable happens, there will be a sense of loss.

In the meantime, I'm going to cherish good old AAA baseball while we have it. I'll be there in the warm sun, cold beer in hand, with Bears fans who are "family." We shall enjoy each other's company in the stands, and the quality of play on the field. We are the ones who really love the sport. We don't need the superstars.

Quote: *The real superstar is a man or woman raising six kids on $150 a week.* — Spencer Haywood.

April 10, 1984

Purists of Denver win name game

INCONSISTENCY.

I hate to start a fight I can't win. Come to think of it, I didn't really start this one. Someone else did, but it doesn't make any difference, I'll lose anyhow. This battle is over a missing apostrophe and a useless "s."

I mentioned Sloan Lake in a recent column. But somewhere between here and the copy desk, an "s" was added to Sloan and it came out Sloans Lake. "You oughtta know better than that!" an angry caller reprimanded me over the telephone. "That's your old neighborhood. You grew up there. It is Sloan Lake, not Sloans Lake."

He is right, of course. The official map of the City and County of Denver lists it as Sloan Lake, and the adjoining body of water on the southeast as Cooper Lake, not Coopers or Cooper's. The lakes were joined in 1940 by a canal, leaving a small island.

The lake was named after Thomas M. Sloan, the farmer who hit an artesian spring in 1860 while digging an irrigation well. Some 200 acres were flooded, according to Judith Allison's book, "Edgewater Four Score." I have no idea who old man Cooper was.

It's true we called it Sloan's Lake when we were kids. But somewhere along the line the apostrophe was dropped.

At the turn of the century, an amusement park called Manhattan Beach was established on the lake. There was an opera house, a small zoo, boathouses and an electric fountain. Frances Melrose, in her "Rocky Mountain Memories" column, noted the name was changed to Luna Park and then back to Manhattan Beach. It finally closed in 1914 because of competition from Elitch's Gardens, not Elitchs Gardens. It is now Elitch Gardens, by the way.

The newspapers can't agree. Marjie Lundstrom wrote an article Jan. 6, 1982, for The Denver Post entitled "Sloan Lake." But Marilyn Holmes, in the April 21 issue, same year, wrote, "Sloans Lake in west Denver is dying . . ." Feb. 28, 1983, Holmes began another story with, "Water skiers and motorboat enthusiasts on Sloan Lake . . ."

We're no better. In the Sept. 14, 1980, issue of the Rocky Mountain News, Jerry Brown wrote: "Using EPA money, the Health Department began testing Sloan Lake this summer to see if it can be cleaned up." But in the April 22, 1982, issue, Burt Hubbard began his story with: "The 116-year-old Sloans Lake recreation area will degenerate into a swamp . . ."

I grudgingly accept the fact that the lake no longer belongs to Sloan and probably should not be called Sloan's Lake. But since it is named after him, why shouldn't we call it Sloan Lake? We don't need the "s." Sloan is not plural.

I have never known who decides these things. It is Pikes Peak, not Pike Peak or Pike's Peak, even though it is Pike National Forest. It is Longs Peak, not Long Peak, but in the same general area it is Hallett Peak, not Halletts Peak.

Is it Washingtons Park, or Barrs Lake, or Big Thompsons River, or Bonnys Reservoir, or Cranmers Park, or Standleys Lake, or Camerons Pass or Martin Luther Kings Boulevard? Nope.

Then it shouldn't be Sloans Lake.

January 27, 1985

What's in a name? Ask any Rojoan

COLORADAN.

Or is it Coloradoan? In the opinion of the late Lee Knous, former governor, it was absolute heresy to refer to a citizen of this state as a Coloradoan. He was a vigorous campaigner on behalf of Coloradan.

Knous lectured me on the subject many years ago during an interview I was conducting with him. Knowing of his Colorado roots, I didn't argue the point. Neither did Palmer Hoyt, then editor and publisher of The Denver Post.

Hoyt — who was an Oregonian, not an Oregonan — became equally convinced Coloradan was the correct spelling. He was so firm in that belief that when The Coloradoan, a daily newspaper in Fort Collins, was mentioned in a story, Post copy editors were told to change the spelling to The Coloradan. I don't think they still misspell it.

The subject came up while I was having dinner at Fort Collins with Jim and Martha Dean. He is now executive editor of The Coloradoan. I asked him about the discrepancy. "We're right and everyone else is wrong," was his quick reply. "When you get back to Denver, you might want to consider this as a cause in your column."

I had almost forgotten about it until I received a letter recently from Robert Hansen, vice president of program and training for the Denver YMCA. It began, "It's beginning to look like Coloradoans may miss out on a once-in-a-lifetime opportunity to support the state's youth programs while becoming a part of history."

The letter was about participation in the 1984 Olympic Torch Relay that will pass through Colorado on its way to Los Angeles in mid-June. But that's not what interested me. It was the way Hansen spelled Coloradoan that caught my eye. Did he know something the rest of us didn't?

I called the Colorado Historical Society to find out which is the correct spelling. "We have no information on the origin of either word," reference librarian Catherine Engle told me. "We have several articles written about the subject but no proof either term is correct."

The problem might have been solved back in 1876 when Colorado, formerly a part of Kansas Territory, was admitted to the Union. Frances Melrose, resident historian here at the News, told me that Idaho really wanted Colorado as its name, but we got it first. I suppose we would have been stuck with Idaho as a name. But then there would have been a debate over whether Idahan or Idahoan was correct.

Most of us who grew up here learned in school that the word Colorado is a Spanish word meaning red. The state got its name, we were told, because of the red rock formations that cut through the state, north to south. First choice in most Spanish dictionaries, however is *rojo.* Second choice is *colorado* and third is *encarnado.*

I suppose we are better off with *colorado* instead of *rojo* or *encarnado.* If we had taken the other two choices, would we have been Rojoans or Rojans? Or would we have been Encarnadoans or Encarnadans?

Heck if I know.

March 20, 1984

5

REASONS
FOR SEASONS

On stuffed robins and hints of spring

Spring had better be on time this year. We aren't the only impatient ones, though. A few anemones, tulips and perennial phlox can't wait. How pleasant to savor the first elusive changes of the seasons.

A crunch of grimy snow from the Thanksgiving Day blizzard remains in a shaded area under one of my blue spruce trees. I'm betting it will still be there the first day of spring.

But that's OK. Blue jays are again chattering in my old cottonwood, and I have already seen swarms of robins. Isn't it exciting to spot the first robin?

That reminds me of a newspaper photographer I knew. He will remain nameless to protect the guilty. My pal always enjoyed the coming of spring and taking pictures of the first robin. And do you know something? He photographed the same robin every year.

Not possible? Yes it was. I know it was the same bird because it was a stuffed robin he carried in the trunk of his car with his cache of other photo props. Late in winter each year, he would take the robin from his car, dust it off and perch it on a snowy tree limb or on a rock in the snow.

I can close my eyes and still see those pictures. That perky little stuffed robin had its head cocked to one side as though listening for a worm wriggling somewhere under the snow.

Another certain sign of spring is the beginning of Young American League baseball practice. Watch the parks late in the afternoon. You'll see little buggers running down fungoes across a muddy field. Along the sidelines, their fathers huddle in the evening chill to talk big, to watch the action and to nurture private dreams of athletic glory for their sons.

If you squint, you will notice a pale green cast to some of the lawns. Out east in the farm country, the stink of fertilizer is heavy in the air, and the sound of farm machinery echoes across empty fields.

"The prairie melts into the throats of larks," as poet Thomas Hornsby Ferril so eloquently wrote, "and green, like water, green flows into the pinto patches of the snow."

Lordy, I wish I had written that.

But for those of us who are not poets, there are relaxed ambles through Bear Creek Park. Small animals, ducks, terns and other water birds are trying to make sense of new sandbars sculpted by the heavy runoff last year. Beavers have come downstream from the mountains and are engineering little dams in the willows.

Have you noticed the nice edge to the morning air? At dawn, the horizon is so close that its texture seems just beyond touch. And even though the great peaks are still snowy, there are unmistakable signs of awakening. Twigs on tree branches bend easily. The soil is black and moist under the mulch.

There may be a specific time when spring arrives. But for me, it is a transitory experience. Every fragile moment is worth cherishing, each subtly different from the one before. The pleasure comes from simply being aware of their existence.

March 13, 1984

In October, we're at our very best

BRIGHT BLUE.

I have often thought that if we had to settle for a single month in Colorado, we could get along just fine with 12 Octobers. We are at our best, our prettiest, our most stimulating. Now is the choicest of our times.

William Bliss Carman said it for me in his "A Vagabond Song" when he wrote:

The scarlet of the maples can shake me like a cry

Of bugles going by.

There is something in October sets the gypsy blood astir.

Our new dog, Oreo, is a mix of frisky breeds. She is mostly black with a white patch on her chest and white tips on her toes and on the end of her long tail. She is a big dog with a lot of puppy still in her, and she hasn't quite managed coordination of her spindly legs. Sometimes they go in one direction as she charges off in another. But how she loves to skitter through clumps of dry leaves in the park!

Oreo doesn't know much about months yet, but I suspect she likes this one because it seems to set her "gypsy blood astir." She doesn't wander too far, though. Oreo enjoys companionship and seems to seek approval when she looks back with one ear perked up and the other flopped down. Have you ever seen a big, black dog with blue eyes?

The mountains shimmer with golden aspens, but the city has its crimson sumac and its yellowing locusts and cottonwoods. The lawns are still deep green and skies are as clear as Chablis.

Great V-formations of Canada geese sweep low over reservoirs at dusk. After the snarl of rush-hour traffic dies to a whisper, you can hear their wings pumping through the chill evening air and their monotone honks echoing into the fading light.

October isn't all sight and sound. It is sometimes an elusive aroma of chili sauce simmering on the stove and being canned, or pickles being put up. You just know that nearby there's a fruit cellar with rows of shiny Ball and Mason jars filled with spiced peaches, apple sass, pickled beets, crisp kosher dills, concord grape conserve and wild plum butter. Lordy!

There is more to October than its pretty face. I think people are nicer and more patient. Strangers are willing to stop to talk of little things just for the sake friendliness. Easy camaraderie replaces guarded indifference.

I do miss the pungent essence of burning leaves. In Denver's innocent past, thin wisps of gray smoke rose from great piles of leaves in back yards. Children roasted russet potatoes in the embers and ate them right on the spot, fire-burned skins and all. It was like camping out.

As the nights lengthen, homes become snug, cozy, warm. And when it's time for rest, the nocturnal air from an open window feels so clean against the face. The comforter is warm, and sleep is swift and sweet.

Quote:

O suns and skies and clouds of June,
And flowers of June together,
Ye cannot rival for one hour
October's bright blue weather.

— Helen Hunt Jackson.

October 14, 1984

Thanksgiving Day

PERISHABLE.

The Idea Fairy had just taken off her tiny Burberry trench coat. She was sitting down on the desk memo pad when I walked into the newsroom.

FAIRY — I thought I'd stop by to see what you are going to write for Thanksgiving Day.

ME — I have been wondering that myself.

FAIRY — You have often said it is your favorite day of the year.

ME — Right. I like the simplicity. No gifts. No trying to buy the affection of family members. It's a time to be together. A time to smell the turkey in the oven. A time to go to sleep on the floor after dinner.

FAIRY — And a time for Trish to work her buns off in the kitchen.

ME — Yes, it's that kind of time, too. But I try to pitch in.

FAIRY — Your legendary turkey stuffing?

ME — Yes. Corn bread, chopped onion, celery, browned country sausage, walnuts, diced Jonathan apples. Maybe some mushrooms.

FAIRY — Why is it you like to cook?

ME — I have thought a lot about that. I suppose there is something to the old adage that he who likes to cook, also likes to eat. But there is more to it than that.

FAIRY — Like what?

ME — As you well know, newspaper columns are very perishable. Same thing with broadcasting. You finish a day's work, and when you look back, you can't see you have really done anything.

FAIRY — Cooking helps you gratify a need for tangible accomplishment?

ME — Sure. And then you get to eat what you have accomplished. That brings us back to the old adage.

FAIRY — Makes sense, I suppose. Whole family coming to your place for dinner?

ME — I wish they were, I miss my kids when I don't see them on Thanksgiving. But we'll have a nice bunch. Six, maybe seven for dinner.

FAIRY — It is a sad day for many.

ME — How do you feel about people eating alone at McDonald's on Thanksgiving Day?

FAIRY — I hurt for them. If they are alone, and they can only have a hamburger for dinner, I hope they at least have a memory of a happier time. You know, when things were better for them. When they were with people who cared about them. And I hope they can look back at all that and not be bitter.

ME — Tough to do when things aren't going your way.

FAIRY — You bet it is. And then there are those who don't even have the memory. I suspect they miss the warmth of a family Thanksgiving Day even though they have never had one.

ME — Do you think people who have never been loved actually miss love?

FAIRY — Oh, Buster, of course they do! You know that. There is a need for love in everyone. That's why Thanksgiving Day is so important. Sure, it's a time to be grateful for the material blessings. But what is even more important, it is a time to be thankful for each other. A time to love and be loved.

ME — And the ones without the memories?

FAIRY — The rest of us just have to work harder to include them in our affection. We must not permit the unloved and unwanted to be isolated from the rest of us.

ME — Big job.

FAIRY — We have to try. Why don't you write a column about that?

ME — I think you just did.

FAIRY — My best to Trish, your mom and the kids.

ME — Happy Thanksgiving Day, Fairy.

FAIRY — Save me a drumstick, OK?

ME — OK.

November 26, 1981

You'll never regret it

CHEERS!

That's what it says on the front of the invitation. Under the top flap, "We're having an open house! Eggnog and munchies. Come see our new condo. Sunday, Dec. 10, 5:00 p.m. until???? Be casual. Barb and Joel. Regrets only."

Down in the corner of the invitation Barb has drawn a little smile-face. Next to it, in parentheses, are the words, "See map."

Sure enough, there's a Xeroxed map folded up in the invitation envelope. You can tell Barb made the map. There's another little smile-face down in the corner.

Under the map, Barb has written, "Take Valley Highway to Hampden. Turn east on Hampden and follow until Hampden becomes Havana. Turn right on Parker Road and keep going southeast until you get to East Yale.

"Turn left on Yale and head east again, crossing I-225, South Pontiac and then Chambers Road. Follow Yale to the northeast until you see the old Pennzoil sign. Keep going 1.7 miles until Yale loops back toward the southwest. Turn north again on Xenophobe Way. Double back on Hollyhock Lane to Yevchenko. South to Sunnyridge Estates. We are in the third cluster, second cul-de-sac, Building C. Cheers!"

Barb adds that if there's any problem, call from the 7-Eleven at East Yonkers Place and South Winnemucca.

Regrets. The word sticks in your mind. You already regret you ever met Barb and Joel. Regret isn't really a strong enough word. Hate. That's it. You hate anything and anybody east of Yosemite.

Damn Barb and Joel.

The snow begins to fall about 2 p.m. Sunday. It's light at first. It really starts coming down by 3:30. At 4, the curbings have disappeared.

That's the way it is when the two of you start out for what you later will describe as "that goddam-cul-de-sac." It will be pitch-dark by the time you get to South Havana. The wind will blow the snow flakes straight into your windshield. You can't see anything.

Your wife is holding the map along with a foil-wrapped fruitcake she is bringing to Barb. Every time you try to stop to look at the map, the idiot behind you blasts away on his horn. You roll down the window and tell him what he can do with his horn.

"Why don't you stop and ask someone," your wife suggests. You tell her to keep her mouth shut, watch the map and tell you when to turn on Xenophobe.

You push on. You are driven like a man possessed by some terrible, unseen devil. Nothing matters but finding the goddam cul-de-sac. You want to tell Joel what a boob he is and to ask him why he can't live on a good, old-fashioned American street like Washington, Gaylord or Pearl.

Your wife puts up with your tantrums for awhile. But she has her limits. The fruitcake got squashed the last time you got out of the car to look at a street sign. She is afraid her deodorant is breaking down and she's almost ready to cry.

Instead, she defiantly takes the tip of her finger and draws a little smile-face on the fogged car window. That does it. You threaten to put her out at the next gas station. She shouts back that if anybody walks home it's going to be you.

You see a light in the distant gloom. You both fall silent as you drive closer. Maybe this is it. Could we have found it? Good old Barb and Joel. It's 8 o'clock. That's not too late. They said 5 p.m. until?, didn't they?

Now you are up to the light. The headlights begin to shine on a sign. At first you can't make out the letters. Then you can see it.

Buckley Air Base.

Forget Barb and Joel. If you ever do get there, the hors d'oeuvres will be gone. The last of the dip will curdled on the bottom of the Lazy Susan.

Avoid this. Telephone your regrets. You won't really regret it. Stay home. Eat the fruitcake. Watch TV. Go to bed early.

Cheers!

December 4, 1978

Rage, rage against dying of the light

LIGHTS.

Sometimes it seems we are as imprisoned by darkness in our time as primordial beings were at the dawn of history. I suppose that is why we illuminate the winter solstice with Christmas and Hanukkah lights.

Decorations we associate with Christmas predate the birth of Jesus Christ. Pagans used fire and light as symbols for warmth and a lasting life. Evergreen trees assured people then as now that life survives in the darkest and coldest of times.

Even though Hanukkah is an eight-day commemoration of the rededication of the Temple by the Macabees after their victory over the Syrians, it occurs during the darkest time of the year and is known as the Jewish Feast of Lights.

Each of us reflects upon ancient events in personal ways. Some see them as prophetic of these times. If there is something we all share, it is an apprehension of the unknown. Though we have become intellectually enlightened, the human spirit still fears the long winter nights.

And why not? The peril of the everlasting darkness of a nuclear holocaust often appears as close as the next nightfall. Ancient prophecies sometimes seem to foreshadow future events. Can it be coincidence that both the old and new hatreds have their roots in the Holy Land?

In today's strife, all parties are slavishly obedient to Old Testament law. As retaliation follows retaliation in Middle East conflicts, we are reminded of Exodus 21:24 — "Eye for eye, tooth for tooth, hand for hand, foot for foot." But vengeance has resolved nothing. It has succeeded only in escalating the fighting. There isn't much cheek turning nowadays.

Was it predictable that these parallels of ancient history and present events would be placed in a biblical context by none other than President Reagan? In a recent interview, he said he had been "musing" about Armageddon, the scene of the final and conclusive battle between good and evil, as foretold in Revelations 16:14-16.

"There have been times in the past when we thought the end of the world was coming, but never anything like this," Reagan said. We have often heard him characterize our side as "good" and the communist side as "evil" in what he perceives as a struggle for world supremacy.

How does one muse about the end of the world? Is it pictured as a dreamy abstraction, or is it the end of light and the beginning of darkness for all things, for every person? Is it a consequence of what we do, or is it an inevitability we can't alter?

Christians must believe the former. The whole idea of Christ being born is based upon hope, not resignation. Christians must believe we are in control of our future and responsible for our actions. That is the light in our darkness. It is our star of Bethlehem.

I suppose the light is not there for those who do not choose to see it. If our president is to muse on Armageddon and its consequences, let him also muse upon the concept of "the fatherhood of God and the brotherhood of man."

That is the stuff of Christianity and the reason we celebrate Christmas.

December 25, 1983

Christmas blues in red and green

GLAZED.

The Idea Fairy had just taken off her tiny L.L. Bean parka. It was folded and placed on my desk calendar. She was softly humming "Jingle Bells" when I walked into the newsroom. A small package was in her lap.

ME — I can tell by that smug look on your face you are ready for Christmas.

FAIRY — The presents are wrapped. Christmas cards have been mailed. My tree is decorated, and I have finished my holiday baking. I brought you something.

ME — Those little date-ball cookies?

FAIRY — Yes. The ones dusted with powdered sugar.

ME — I love those date-ball cookies. Chewy, nutty and almost as good as your fruitcake. The worst piece of your fruitcake I have ever tasted was superlative.

FAIRY — For someone who professes not to like Christmas, you certainly enjoy the fringe benefits.

ME — I don't dislike the idea of Christmas. The part I don't like is trying to buy the affection of others with presents that don't fit them or they don't want.

FAIRY — Not true, Buster. You play that game all year long. It's the shopping you don't like.

ME — That's certainly part of it.

FAIRY — You would do well to start early. But you wait until the last minute and then your eyes become glazed. In a state of panic, you go out and indiscriminately throw money at department store clerks and expect the true spirit of Christmas to survive.

ME — It's shopping malls I don't like. How degrading it is to stagger home late at night, reeking of Orange Julius and Karmel Korn. I hate it when people leave their half-eaten hot dogs in those sand-filled cigarette urns.

FAIRY — And . . .

ME — And the floors are sticky from spilled Pepsi. Kids insist on running down the escalators the wrong way. There is row after row of identical pink and green argyle acrylic sweaters. Fredericks of Hollywood has little red bikini Christmas panties. I can't find the restrooms. No one waits on me. I can't remember where I parked the car.

FAIRY — Other than that?

ME — Other than that there is nothing I like about Christmas shopping.

FAIRY — Have you sent a letter to Santy with a list of what you want?

ME — It's Santa, not Santy. And no, there is nothing special I want for Christmas. I always send a letter telling Santa what I don't want. This year I don't want a "swinger" inversion exerciser.

FAIRY — How about a telephone answering tape recorder?

ME — Nope, and I also don't want a digital watch, men's cologne or a box of California dried figs.

FAIRY — Maybe someone will give you an electric fondue set or maybe a 1,400-watt hair dryer.

ME — I need a hair dryer like I need more arthritis.

FAIRY — Then what do you want?

ME — Just pass the date-ball cookies, please.

December 15, 1983

Memories linger of a lonely Christmas

A CHRISTMAS PAST.

William Austin Huggins writes from Madison, Wis., about the loneliness of Christmas. "It was cold that night in Denver, the kind of cold that sweeps down from the Colorado Rockies and digs deep into one's bones. What snow there was rested in small clumps in areas protected from the wind or bounced along the street like little frightened insects on the run."

The year was 1911. Huggins was 15 then, a runaway from his home in Oklahoma. "Lights from the stores sent beams out onto the sidewalk," he recalled, "and package-laden Denverites, each intent on some personal business, didn't linger in the cold air."

Huggins remembers being all wrapped up in the holiday spirit. He was old enough to run away. Young enough to yearn for the magic of a child's Christmas.

"I felt the cold as I wandered aimlessly along Curtis Street, knowing that as a stranger in Denver, I wouldn't see a familiar face. I was willing to endure the cold just to escape the barren loneliness of my small hotel room."

Huggins was hungry. He had just enough money for one meal. What to do? Eat now or try to wait until the next day? The boy was out of work. There weren't many jobs in the winter of 1911.

As Huggins tried to decide what to do, he found himself in front of a men's clothing store. In the window were shirts, shoes, socks and other furnishings. He remembers exactly how he felt.

"As I looked I could hear all about me the men and women scurrying along, laughing and talking and all seemingly filled with happiness and good cheer. Somehow I began to feel my loneliness more and more. I didn't belong to anyone here. I was a stranger in a strange land and all the others were playing a game in which I was not included."

Huggins is 82 now. He is retired. Behind him is a long career as a newspaperman for the Philadelphia Bulletin, Atlanta Constitution, Daily Oklahoman, Oklahoma News and the San Diego Sun. Huggins admits to a few ailments, ". . . but they are overshadowed by my interest in writing."

There have been a lot of deadlines since 1911 for Huggins. How many stories? Too many to remember. But Huggins never forgot the one about himself. As memory reaches out across the years, he can still see that cold and hungry boy, standing in front of the new store on Curtis Street.

"Suddenly, I knew what I had to do.

"Glancing once more at the store window, I strode through the door and made my way through the throng inside.

"Twenty minutes later, I was back in my hotel room again. This time something had been added, something small and inexpensive but just the necessary touch for the occasion."

We can almost see the boy. The room must have been small. Probably a porcelain basin and pitcher on the nightstand. Gideon Bible in the dresser drawer. Young Huggins took off his coat. He was so alone.

"I placed the 'something' on the dresser and stepped across the room to look at it. What did it matter that I was the only one to see it? Didn't it make me a player in the game?"

He must have been thinking of his home in Oklahoma. And certainly there were thoughts of those he had left behind. Were they thinking of him? Did they remember?

"I walked slowly to the dresser and picked up the 'something,' knowing that its purchase had taken all my money except for a few cents. I ran my hand over the colorful wrapping and slowly began removing the bright ribbons and little green balls. I lifted the lid on the box inside and took out a green pair of bedroom slippers and the card."

There wasn't any Christmas tree in that hotel room. There were no carols. The aroma of roasting turkey wasn't in the air. No children. Just a boy. Alone.

He took the card carefully out of the gift box and held it to the light. It said —

"Merry Christmas from Me to Me."

December 25, 1978

Peace on Earth

THE CITY IS QUIET NOW. SHOPPING CENTER MALLS ARE EMPTY. TRAFFIC signals downtown are like lonely sentinels standing guard over empty streets. There is darkness behind store windows.

Out in the neighborhoods, people scurry through the cold to trash cans with great, crumpled wads of holiday wrapping paper. New bicycles are wobbling along sidewalks. A troubled man climbs wearily into his car and wonders where he'll find D cell batteries on Christmas morning.

The smells of incense, new clothing and cologne mingle in the church. "Hodie Christus Natus Est" echoes down on a fidgety little boy. An infant cries and is hurried from the pew and down the aisle.

The hospital room is quiet, but for the measured wheeze of the little old man asleep on a high, white bed. There is a tube in his nose. On a corner table is a small, plastic Christmas tree. Outside the door, the nurse's shoes squeak rapidly along the empty hall. She frets that there was no time to bake fruitcake or Christmas cookies this year. There is a distant laugh from an opening elevator door.

The kitchen windows of the old north Denver house are fogged with steam. The lights inside are bright and the woman bends over and cracks the oven door. There's a rush of sweet sage aroma. Now, she opens the oven all the way and bastes the breast, legs and wings of the turkey with a plastic syringe.

There's an old Chevy scraping along Kalamath at West 12th Avenue. The six youths inside are restless and don't know where to go. The runner along the Highline Canal pulls his knit cap down around his ears.

It is Christmas and we don't have to get ready for it anymore. Not for another year. There were private moments this past week that were filled with sadness. On the crowded streets were the lonely for whom fulfillment always seems to fall short of promise. The price of humanness is never greater than at Christmastime.

For the little girl, though, it was difficult to contain her joy. She ran and skipped and impulsively kissed her mother on the cheek. And then her tiny, sticky hand found its way into her father's hand.

The plain, young woman in her east Denver apartment leafed aimlessly through a magazine. She kept looking at the telephone. It wouldn't ring. It just plain wouldn't ring.

A sweet-faced minister on television asked, "Where is he that is born King of the Jews? For we have seen his star in the East, and are come to worship him."

He was in a manger. There had been no room at the inn. There are plenty of rooms at the Holiday Inn this morning and there aren't very many people in the coffee shop.

The parking lots at Mile High Stadium are empty now. A chill wind swirls scraps of litter against the chain link fence. No one is in the stadium. It waits patiently for future cheers.

Worshipers heap symbols upon ancient rituals and expect a miracle of joy. And for some, it works. There's nothing better than frankincense and myrrh. Unless maybe it's a stereo or a deluxe two-in-one toaster oven. And listen, there's a lot of good will and good cheer in just one more toddy for the road.

The road to Christmas is long. It seems to be just over there, under that star. Sometimes it seems so close, close enough to touch.

Is it Christmas when the child touches the bright star on the tree? Is it Christmas when the time runs out and the presents go unwrapped? Is it Christmas when the last drops of white port are gone from the bottle in the paper sack?

It is Christmas now.

The road doesn't end here. It starts here. It is the beginning. We start here, under this star. We find peace on Earth and high in a winter sky. There is good will in the smile of a stranger. We take gifts from the manger and the greatest of these is love.

The infant is life. We feel a special reverence for birth. The life we celebrate now is such a fragile, lovely thing. We have found our joy.

Joy to the world!

December 25, 1977

6

SAUCES AND OTHER SPICY STUFF

Main dish was worth the wait

Suspense.

The moment of truth came three hours after the terracotta roaster went into the oven. In clay cookery, peeking under the lid is a no-no. And after spending an hour preparing it, we didn't want anything to happen to our *poulet aux quarante gousses d'ail.*

When the lid was lifted, there was no disappointment. That big, fat, 6½-pound chicken that had been roasted with 40 cloves of garlic was beautiful, aromatic and ready.

Forty cloves of garlic?

Yes. My daughter, Muffy, had prepared it for Trish and me a couple of years ago. I liked it so much Muffy gave me a clay roaster as a gift. But I had never used it until Sunday. Muffy had come by to watch the Broncos-Chargers game on television with us and said she would teach me.

I made the dressing while Muffy was peeling the garlic cloves. Both the top and bottom of the clay roaster had been soaked for a half-hour in lukewarm water. The game began and Rich Karlis booted a 44-yard field goal on Denver's first possession.

Meanwhile, I was browning the bird in a heavy skillet with a cup of olive oil seasoned with a bay leaf and one teaspoon each of sage, rosemary and thyme. I stuffed the bird and as I was lacing up its south end, Dan Fouts was connecting with Charlie Joiner for a 25-yard scoring pass with 5:37 left in the first quarter. San Diego 7, Denver 3.

Muffy and I put the chicken along with six peeled carrots, two quartered onions and the 40 cloves of garlic into the clay pot. Then we drizzled half the olive oil over the whole works, adding all the sage, rosemary, thyme and bay leaf which had been strained from the oil. The Broncos settled for a 45-yard Karlis field goal. San Diego 7, Denver 6.

We put the roaster in a cold oven, turned it on at 350, and I started to clean up the olive oil that had spattered over everything. Late in the second period, San Diego's Rolf Benirschke booted a 49-yard field goal, making the score 10-6.

At halftime, I took my dog, Yazzie, to the park for his afternoon walk. When we got back in the car, it was the third period and KOA's Bob Martin reported that Karlis had missed a 34-yard field goal attempt.

There was a marvelous aroma in the house when we came home. Denver and San Diego exchanged field goals again, making the score 13-9. Then in the last 38 seconds, John Elway moved the Broncos to the 1-yard-line and Sammy Winder scored Denver's only touchdown. Benirschke missed a 46 yarder in the game's final 8 seconds and Denver won 16-13.

While the game's only suspense came in the final minute, suspense on the bird had been mounting all afternoon. At the final gun, Trish made the gravy. We opened the roaster, and the chicken was superb.

The secret, of course, is not to crush or mince the garlic but to cook it whole. The flavor is warm and mild, and the cooked garlic is delicious when spread like butter on French bread.

There is a recipe for 40-clove chicken using a conventional roaster in Suzanne McLucas excellent cookbook, "A Provencal Kitchen in America."

We call ours the San Diego Chicken.

November 13, 1984

Hit man Valachi's meatballs live on

MAFIA MEATBALLS.

A copy of my book "Morning," has made its way to Washington, D.C., and into the hands of Carl Coleman, an old pal from my days at Channel 7. He later worked at the Time-Life news bureau in the nation's capital.

Prompted by my recipe in the book for Uncle Geno's North Side Spicy Meatballs, Coleman sent me a copy of a recipe for spaghetti and meatballs concocted by the late Mafia hit man, Joe Valachi.

"It is in Joe Valachi's own words as told to Time-Life correspondent Lance Lamont, who had spent a day at the old D.C. jail interviewing Valachi for a Time cover story," Coleman's letter said.

The underworld executioner was being held in Washington to testify before Sen. John McClellan's permanent investigations subcommittee in 1963. Valachi had broken a blood oath to testify about the workings of the Cosa Nostra and was under a death sentence from the mob.

No one ever collected the $100,000 price on Valachi's head. He died in 1971 of a heart attack while serving a life sentence at the La Tuna federal prison in Texas. That's where he was being held under federal protection from underworld reprisal.

Valachi may be dead, but his meatballs live on. In his own words, here is the recipe:

"Now follow everything I am going to tell you. You will use one cup of the bread crumbs for each pound of chopped meat. In fact, if you buy a pound of lean beef, and grind it yourself, that's better because you will know that the meat is fresh. Let's say you are going to make meatballs from one pound of chopped meat, then you use the one cup of bread crumbs.

"This is the most important thing I am going to tell you. Spread the bread crumbs on a board. Don't mix it with the meat until I tell you. Break two eggs into the crumbs. Put in three pieces (cloves) of garlic chopped very fine. A quarter teaspoon of pepper and the same amount of salt. Next put in a teaspoon of oregano and a quarter pound of grated Romano cheese. Pour a little less than a cup of milk and mix it all together with your hands until it is mixed and good and damp.

"Take the chopped meat and mix it all together until you can't see the crumbs and other stuff. All you should see is the meat. When that is done, put some olive oil in a small dish, and as you roll the meat in the palms of your hands, you keep putting a little olive oil on the palms so the meat won't stick. You can make meatballs any size you want. I usually make them the size of a lime.

"Now go get a frying pan and put about four tablespoons of olive oil in the pan. Add half a chopped onion, one piece (clove) of garlic and as many meatballs as you want. Don't try and turn the meatballs until they are cooked or they will stick to the pan. You kind of 'feel' each one as you turn it and if it sort of sticks then leave it alone until it turns easily. You let them cook halfway or half done with the onion and garlic . . . then take them out and set them aside until you have them all cooked."

Next: Valachi's sauce, and the "soldier" goes to the "mattress."

January 10, 1984

Valachi's sauce no kiss of death

MOP UP.

When Joe Valachi was held in the Washington, D.C., jail 20 years ago, he prepared his own meals. He was isolated from other prisoners during his appearance before a congressional investigations subcommittee.

About six weeks before Valachi's testimony, the Justice Department revealed that he had been providing the FBI information about the underworld Cosa Nostra (Our Thing) and termed his help "an extraordinarily important intelligence breakthrough."

As a result, Mafia boss Vito Genovese gave Valachi "the kiss of death" and ordered him killed. A $100,000 price was put on his head. For this reason, Valachi was unable to mingle with other prisoners and did his own cooking on a small hot plate in his jail cell.

It was there that Time-Life correspondent Lance Lamont interviewed Valachi for a Time cover story. In the process of confessing participation to murders, dope dealing and being "the best Shylock in town," the old mobster also spilled out his own recipe for spaghetti and meatballs. It was sent to me by an old pal, former Time-Life staffer Carl Coleman, now a public relations spokesman for the Department of Health and Human Services in Washington, D.C.

The meatball part of the recipe was in this column Tuesday. In Valachi's words, here is his recipe for the sauce.

"Now go get a four-quart pot and a large can of 'Pepe' or similar brand of Italian plum tomatoes. Dump the tomatoes into the pot and add two small cans of tomato paste. Put in half a can of water. Use the can the tomatoes came in. Put in one-quarter teaspoon of sugar, one tablespoon of salt, one teaspoon of black pepper, one head (clove) garlic and one teaspoon of oregano.

"Cover the pot and let it boil very slowly for an hour. After this, take the cover off the pot and let it boil slowly for another hour or so to let the water steam out of the tomatoes. Let it boil for about two hours all-told.

"Strain the sauce in a pasta strainer. Use a flat-bottomed glass to smash the sauce through the strainer so that it will all go into another pot. You will have the taste of the onions and garlic, resulting in a very smooth sauce."

At this point, Valachi suggested you add the previously prepared meatballs to the sauce. Simmer until the meatballs are cooked all the way through.

For pasta, the old mosbter recommended "Perciatelli No. 6." He has special instructions for its preparation as well:

"When you cook your pasta, make sure you put some salt into the pot and some olive oil so it won't stick together. I think you should use grated Romano cheese with the dinner and drink an Italian table wine when you are eating. You also need Italian bread to mop up the sauce.

"It is very good, and I used to make it when I was a 'soldier' and we had to go to the 'mattress' (a ritual prelude to gang warfare).

Despite Valachi's prediction that he would die by "the knife and gun," he lived out his life by the "fork and spoon" under government protection at the La Tuna federal prison in Texas. He died there of a heart attack April 3, 1971.

January 12, 1984

Making amends for the 'hit sauce'

CONFESSION.

Remember that recipe I gave you for mobster Joe Valachi's spaghetti sauce? Some readers thought it was terrible. One reader suggested that the old Mafia hit man must have rubbed out his victims by forcing them to eat the stuff.

I have no idea what went wrong. As you may recall, the recipe was really hearsay. I obtained it third-hand from an old pal of mine in Washington, D.C., who in turn got it from a Time-Life reporter, who supposedly got it from Valachi during a prison interview.

Somewhere in all that, there must have been a slip between Valachi's cup and your lip. *Chi lo sa?* Who knows? I confess I never tried it, but because of the hostile mail, I resolved to come up with a spaghetti sauce suitable for robust autumn appetites.

The most important ingredient is mood. Do not mince a single garlic clove or take a sip of Chianti until your mood is Italian. Sit down, close your eyes and listen to Luciano Pavarotti's recording of *E lucevan le stelle* from Puccini's "Tosca."

Now you mince the garlic clove, combining it with one small, finely chopped onion in a 4-quart pot. Saute until transparent over low heat in four tablespoons of olive oil. What an aroma! Add two 16-

ounce cans of peeled tomatoes that have been pulsed a couple of times in a blender. Don't puree. Leave the tomatoes a little chunky.

I have tried this recipe with blanched and peeled fresh tomatoes, but frankly, it just isn't as good as with canned tomatoes.

You might want to try Pomi, a new product imported from Italy. It is crushed and strained fresh tomatoes in a box containing 35 fluid ounces. No preservatives or seasoning. Great stuff, but it doesn't make the sauce as chunky as canned tomatoes.

Add one 15-ounce can of tomato sauce and two 6-ounce cans of tomato paste. Sprinkle two teaspoons of sweet basil and a pinch of oregano. Next comes one teaspoon of pepper. If you like your sauce *con fuoco*, give it three generous shakes of Tabasco sauce.

Stir in three tablespoons of minced parsley and some sliced fresh mushrooms and simmer over low heat for about two hours. *Da tempo al tempo.*

You'll note that the sauce is quite thick and plops as it cooks. It can be thinned with water, but try V-8 Cocktail or Mott's Clamato juice.

You can make subtle changes in the flavor by adding a pinch of rosemary, savory, thyme, sage or marjoram. But try it this way first.

If you don't make your own pasta, or don't have a favorite noodle, put Uncle Geno's North Side Spaghetti Sauce over DaVinci fettucine. Serve it, of course, with Uncle Geno's North Side Spicy Meatballs, the recipe for which is on page 210 of "Morning," a modest collection of my columns, modestly priced at $7.95 and available at most book stores.

As you can see, modesty is not one of my virtues, but zippy spaghetti sauce is. Forget the sauce of the old *padrone. Basta!* Enough. Time to put on the Pavarotti and to mince the garlic.

Alla vostra salute!

September 18, 1984

A duel — recipes at 20 paces or so

SCRAPPLE.

Did you see that shot Mal Deans took at me in the Commentary section of the Sunday Rocky Mountain News? Unbelievable! Our readers' representative has savaged me not for something I have written, but for something he thinks I *may* write.

Deans is a senior instructor at the University of Colorado School of Journalism and a former assistant managing editor of the Philadelphia Bulletin. He writes a weekly column answering readers' complaints about how news is handled in the Rocky Mountain News.

Personable as Mal is, when he walks through the newsroom, reporters skitter out of his way like chickens when a fox gets in the hen house. No one likes to be stuck for an inadvertent little inaccuracy or occasional lapse in fairness.

Since he and I are in the same general age group — I may be a shade older — we often swap curmudgeonly views. When talk came around to the importance of a robust breakfast, I recommended he try my recipe for corned beef hash. He in turn introduced me to scrapple, a dish he somehow learned to like in his native Philadelphia.

OK, so my corned beef hash recipe doesn't seem to hold much promise at first glance. It is quite simple. Take a can of any brand of corned beef hash, break it up and add chopped kosher dill pickles and chopped pickled herring. Brown in a skillet and nest poached eggs thereon.

Marvelous! I have it once or twice a month. It's salty, nicely textured. Pleasant aftertaste. It is an ambitious little hash. You will be amused by its impertinence.

Deans' scrapple, however, is not fit for human consumption. Let me quote from the wrapper: "Pork stock, pork, pork skins, pork livers, wheat flour, pork fat, pork hearts, salt, spices."

Scrapple reminds me of a stew drovers ate on early West cattle drives. It was called "cowboy s.o.b." and was made of what was left of the steer after all the edible portions were butchered away. That's the kind of early West lore you didn't get on Gov. Richard D. Lamm's TV program, "Real West."

There are some things in life you don't want to know. You don't want to know your daughter is living with the lead singer in a punk rock group. You don't want to know how much sugar is in ketchup. You don't want to know John Coit wears an earring. And you certainly don't want to know what is in scrapple. You don't want to eat it, either.

With my corned beef hash, you know what's in it. But with scrapple, you know there are pig parts, but what parts? Lordy, I don't know and I don't want to know.

In a clear case of prior restraint, Deans wrote, "If Capt. Gourmet touts *Corned Beef Hash Mit Pickles Und Herring* in his column, turn the page fast."

So you see, he did stick it to me before the fact. But because of my admiration of him, I decided to go ahead and give the recipe, not only to protect his integrity, but to share something delicious with you.

Quote: *I have never eaten scrapple, but I have stepped in it now and again.* — Nosmo King.

January 8, 1985

Hold the pickles

PICKLES.

Sunday wasn't the best of days. It started out at 7 a.m. when my mother called to say a leaky pipe had flooded her upstairs bathroom, the living room below and the basement below that.

You know how those things are. Wallpaper stained. Mops and buckets. Plumbers. The whole shot. We finally got things pretty well blotted up shortly before noon.

I decided to devote the afternoon to working on a ham loaf recipe. I love ham loaf. The best ham loaf I have ever tasted was made by Del Plested. She and I worked together in broadcasting. That was before she became Denver correspondent for Women's Wear Daily.

Anyhow, I puttered around the kitchen for a couple of hours. There was a nice piece of Smithfield ham left over from last week. I ground it up with some fresh veal and pork. You know the rest: a couple of eggs, bread crumbs, spices, mustard and brown sugar glaze, pineapple juice.

Something about it didn't look quite right. It was skimpy. Had no authority. It just sat there. What the heck, I thought, I'll go ahead and finish it. Maybe it will taste better than it looks.

I had planned on making a sauce *veloute* with whipped cream, chicken stock and a lot of other goodies. But, I reasoned, it would be foolish to put a superb sauce on mediocre ham loaf. So, I slipped down to Bear Valley King Soopers to get some store-bought horseradish sauce.

On the shelf below the sauce I noticed a row of Vlasic sweet butter chips. They are about as close to home-canned bread and butter pickles you can get these days. So, I picked up a jar. After getting a box of dishwasher detergent, I headed for the express checkout line.

I must have looked pretty raunchy. It was probably the faded corduroys and the old Harry Hoffman's T-shirt I was wearing. Hadn't shaved because of the plumbing problem.

As the lady before me was paying her check, I began to juggle my three items so I could reach in my pocket for money. I glanced behind me and noted how long the two express lines were getting. That was my mistake. In the process, I lost the pickles. They smashed on the floor.

I could feel the hostility of those behind me. And, why not? They were in a hurry. People were standing there with melting ice cream in their hands. A poor guy had probably dashed out for a bottle of ketchup while his steaks were on the grill, and some bimbo has to drop his pickles.

The young checkout woman managed a brave little smile. She then picked up her microphone and said, "WET CLEANUP ON EXPRESS TWO!" Her voice boomed throughout the store. I just know everyone there turned around to look at the bimbo who dropped his pickles.

I stooped over and picked up the lid. "It's $1.03," I whispered. "I broke it. I'll pay for it. I'm terribly sorry. Take my money and I'll get out of here."

"No," she said, "I'll get you another jar. What were they, Vlasic's sweet butter chips, 16 ounce?"

She disappeared. The line behind me stirred restlessly. People just joining the line were craning to see the bimbo who dropped his pickles.

Finally the checker came back with another jar of sweet butter chips. "It's a terrible mess," I said, looking down at the broken glass, the scattered pickles and my sticky shoes. "I'll be glad to clean it up," I added.

She managed another brave smile. "Not to worry. That jar of pickles was never intended to be eaten. It was destined to be broken. If you hadn't have dropped those pickles, someone else would have."

I paid my check and started to walk out the store. The crepe rubber soles on my shoes had absorbed the pickle juice. My footsteps sounded, "schlock, schlock, schlock." Everyone was looking at the bimbo.

Ham loaf was too dry. Needed a sauce *veloute.*

June 16, 1981

It's your turn, ketchup squirters

FWOP! FWOP!

That's the sound of a man furiously pounding the bottom of a ketchup bottle with the palm of his hand. He pounds and he pounds, and all of a sudden — SPLAT! Out comes a glob of ketchup the size of a meadow muffin.

The H.J. Heinz Co. has addressed this problem. The solution is a plastic squeeze container that forever does away with the anger and frustration of not being able to get the ketchup out of the bottle and onto the french fries.

"It's an attempt to bury another American institution," thundered a senior newsroom curmudgeon. "Are we getting so soft we can't even pound the bottom of ketchup bottles? This is the worst idea since the battery-powered pepper mill.

"And how will the tables and counters in diners look when the familiar glass bottles are replaced by red plastic jars with spouts on top? They'll look like the counters next to the hot dog stands at Mile High. Arraugh!"

Even though I am also something of a traditionalist, I must disagree with the senior newsroom curmudgeon. I guess I have wound up with a lapful of ketchup too many times. The Heinz people have a better idea and I salute them for it.

I was once told the way to accelerate ketchup flow from a newly opened bottle was to hold it at an angle with the left hand and lightly tap the neck with the right forefinger. Doesn't work. I usually resort to inserting the handle of a spoon into the opening. But then I never know what to do with a spoon that has ketchup slathered all over the handle.

The Heinz company may have problems instructing people on how to use the new container. After years of being told, "Don't squeeze the Charmin," consumers will be re-educated to "Squeeze the bottle."

The new Heinz plastic container resembles bottles used by some brands of shampoo. It has a little pop-up spout on top. I won't buy shampoo with any other type of closure.

I don't give a hoot about pH values, scent, conditioners or dandruff-fighting ingredients. Give me something I can open and close in the shower with slippery wet hands. How many times have you tried to chase down a screw top to a shampoo bottle that is skittering around on the shower floor?

Speaking of containers, I am delighted to announce that contrary to information contained in an earlier column, the Royal Crest Dairy does indeed still market some of its milk products in glass bottles. A nice young man came to my home and introduced me to a product called Royal Rich Natural.

I'm getting it now from my home-delivery man. It is indeed rich with butterfat and is a marked improvement over that thin watery low-cal stuff skinny ladies drink these days.

Getting back to plastic containers, now that Heinz has solved the ketchup-flow problem, maybe it is ready to develop a technology to remove the last two Spanish olives wedged at the bottom of their tube-like containers.

Quote: *It is the nature of man as he grows older ... to protest against change, particularly change for the better.* — John Steinbeck.

May 13, 1984

No camouflage for corn willy

SURPRISE.

We are coming up soon on the 40th anniversary of my corn willy recipe. We have already had the 40th anniversary of D-day, the Battle of the Bulge, the capture of Iwo Jima and the crossing of the Rhine at Remagen.

Now it is time to commemorate one of the great culinary catastrophes of World War II. It is a painful memory because I perpetrated the atrocity. It was not intentional, but like "friendly fire," it was nonetheless destructive.

I didn't find war the noble experience that some brass hats have described. By and large, war is mostly a bunch of confused guys bumping into each other. Wars are won by armies with fire power and blind luck.

Soldiers spend their time in either a state of terror or boredom. I can still see those pathetic World War II doggies, hunkered down, reading the labels of C-ration cans as though they had been written by Ernest Hemingway. That's boredom.

I thought of all this when Pat Hanna, our food editor, gave me an unofficial MRE (Meal, Ready-to-Eat) cookbook for GIs in today's Army. Lightweight, nutritious MRE rations are thermal-processed chow originally developed for astronauts. The McIlhenny Co. gives away the cookbook with the purchase of each authentic-looking camouflage holster containing a bottle of its famous Tabasco pepper sauce.

How I wish we would have had something like that to jazz up the three C-ration menus we had: meat and beans, meat and vegetable stew and meat and vegetable hash. Gassy.

The K-rations could have used a little help, too. Did you ever eat canned scrambled eggs, or canned American processed cheese or, worst of all, canned corned pork loaf with carrot bits and apple flakes?

The worst of the field rations was canned corned beef. To World War I doughboys, it was bully beef. We called it corn willy. Whatever you called it, it didn't bear the slightest resemblance to real corned beef. It was more like Ken-L-Ration.

One dull day in the Saar 40 years ago, I tried to disguise corn willy's distinctive taste. I added a chopped onion and a can of corned pork loaf. I mixed in some spuds, an old carrot and a can of meat and vegetable hash. I put the whole works in a steel helmet and stirred it with a bayonet. I sliced some of that rubbery K-ration cheese, put it on top and covered everything with ground-up hardtack. Then I nestled the helmet down in the embers of our fire.

A colonel came by about an hour later. "Smells mighty good, soldier. I'll have some of that. What do you call it?" he asked.

"I call it 'sergeant's surprise,' sir."

I spooned some of it out in my aluminum canteen cup. The old man shoveled it down his gullet. He started to chew after about the third spoonful. His face turned red, he coughed and spat my casserole on the ground.

"CORN WILLY!" he thundered.

"Surprised?" I asked.

After he finally cleared his throat, he looked at me for a moment and said, "I think you ought to change the name of it."

"Sir?"

"Yes, how about 'sergeant's revenge'?"

March 14, 1985

7

HIGH-TECH TALK

On shacking up with a computer

ALONE.

Dorothy left me. She walked out and is never coming back. Dorothy said she was going to California and that we'll never see each other again. You don't know how terribly alone I feel now that she is gone.

Dorothy Huwe was my computer teacher. Our eyes met across the crowded Radio Shack Education Center classroom. I knew then how important she would be in my life. I had no idea, though, how really dependent on her I would become during our short, bittersweet relationship.

It was one of those chance things. I had called Radio Shack to see if there were any classes offered on their SuperSCRIPSIT word processing program. I was assigned to Dorothy's class. It was there she patiently guided me through the world of Header Pages, Viewer Modes, Cursor Movement Commands and Wraparound.

Oh, I know, you think it was my first affair with computers, but you are wrong. I had been fooling around with a trim little Model 100 TRS-80. We even went to San Francisco and Dallas last summer to cover the political conventions. Sometimes we'd be up half the night, just interfacing our brains out.

You know how these summertime flings are. Maybe a little wild and crazy, but soon forgotten. This thing Dorothy and I had was not kid stuff. It was the real thing.

Dorothy told me at the end of my last lesson that she was leaving Radio Shack and moving to the West Coast. "You can't do that!" I cried. "Who can I turn to when I need to make Hyphenation Decisions?"

"Look," she said with that reassuring smile of hers, "you'll be fine. Before long, you'll be making a Global Search and will be able to change the Verify Deletions Default all by yourself. You'll forget about me in no time."

"You mean I can't even call you and ask how to Execute and Display Block-Action Commands?" I mumbled.

"No," she said quietly but firmly.

"Goodbye," I said.

"Goodbye, Geno. Don't forget to remove your diskettes from both drives before you shut down the machine."

And that was it. The other night, though, I woke up from a terrible dream screaming, "ASCII! ASCII! What does it mean?"

And then I heard Dorothy's quiet voice in my mind. My heart began to pound. She was saying, "ASCII stands for American Standard Code for Information Interchange."

Sleep was impossible then. I got up, sponged cold water on my face and sat down before my TRS-80 Model 4, my DMP400 printer and my acoustic modem. I inserted the Vidtex diskette and punched "SET *CL TO COM/DVR." And then, "ENTER."

My mouth was dry and my palms sweaty, but within moments I was interfacing with CompuServe and reading the Dow Jones stock averages. Lordy! Next, I am going to Upload. Wouldn't Dorothy be proud?

Thank you, Dorothy. Then I heard her voice in my mind again. "Don't forget to punch 'CTRL Q' and 'E' to exit. Remember to remove both diskettes from the drives before shutting down."

You know something, Dorothy, sometimes you can be a real nag.

February 12, 1985

Who knows what evil lurks . . .

CHATTERBOX.

The old man was near death. Attendants at the nursing home had been maintaining an around-the-clock vigil after it was learned he was the last person who could remember when there was no television.

The number of pre-TV survivors had been declining rapidly in recent years. As the old man's final moments drew near, he opened his clouded eyes and feebly motioned to a nurse that he had something to say.

Those around his bedside leaned forward to hear the old man's last words. Very clearly, he said, "Who's a little chatterbox? The one with pretty auburn locks? Cute little she. That's Little Orphan Annie."

And then he slipped away. Articles were published about his death. Social scientists debated the meaning of his last words, finally dismissing them as senile ramblings.

That scenario popped into my mind during a recent sleepless night. On a radio newscast, I heard about a survey that found only 30 percent of people now living have any recollection of America before television.

In some ways, those years seem like yesterday. On balance, I would have to say they were happier times, given the absence from our lives of "The Jeffersons," "Punky Brewster," "Three's a Crowd," "Facts of Life," "Dallas" and most of the rest of our daily TV fare. I would trade the whole works for a single Ovaltine-sponsored episode of "Little Orphan Annie" on the radio.

As our number dwindles, I suppose we are the last people able to keep television separate in our minds from reality. For us, TV has remained an advanced entertainment technology. For the other 70 percent of Americans, it has been an electronic information environment into which they were born and have always lived.

The consequences of television are immeasurable. Jane Fonda had little to do with ending the Vietnam War. Watching massacres mixed with deodorant commercials during dinner-hour TV newscasts stripped America of its invulnerability and created the climate that ended the war.

There is no doubt that television advanced the civil rights revolution by at least a century. We all know too much about each other for old racial barriers to be maintained.

All of that is to the good. What worries me is that an increasing number of people today are unable to draw the line between fact and fiction of what they see on television. It has all become entertainment, even the recent hostage crisis in Lebanon. America loves to tie yellow ribbons around trees. The terrible famine in Ethiopia is remembered for the gathering of rock stars and "We are the world. We are the children."

The so-called docu-drama, or fictional account of a real event, is another example of how history can be twisted to enhance dramatic impact. We should have anticipated this when Orson Welles frightened America in 1938 with his "The War of the Worlds" dramatization on the old "Mercury Theater on the Air" radio series.

Even so, it seems to me we had a better handle on keeping fact and fiction in perspective before TV. Perhaps the adage "seeing is believing" is more deeply ingrained than we imagined.

But it won't be long until the 30 percent of us who can tell the difference will be gone. And then it won't matter.

Or will it?

July 9, 1985

Phone solicitors leave us touched

CELLULAR.

I had hoped that when the government broke up the telephone monopoly, it would be more difficult to reach out and touch me. Not so. I'm getting more telephone calls than ever, and I wish they would stop.

Fat chance. I received a call the other night from a young man who informed me that I had just won a free home solar-energy feasibility study. He asked when it would be convenient to come out to deliver my prize.

"We've won?" I shouted incredulously as I cupped my hand over the telephone. "Trish, Susan, come in here! Listen to this. A man on the telephone has just told me we have won a free home solar-energy feasibility study!"

Gee whiz! What an embarrassment of riches! I can't believe it. How lucky can you get?

Susan started jumping up and down and clapping her hands. Trish was hugging me and laughing and crying all at the same time. We were deliriously happy at our good fortune.

But then, as is so often the case, our feelings of elation gave way to those of remorse and guilt. We just plain didn't deserve to win. Our cup had runneth over. Trish looked at me and I looked at her. There was no need to speak.

"Sir," I mumbled into the telephone as I blinked away the tears, "Don't think us ungrateful, but we must decline our prize of a free home solar-energy feasibility study.

"Please," I said as he tried to interrupt. "The little lady and I have received so many blessings recently, it just wouldn't be fair. Give the free home solar-energy feasibility study to a more deserving family."

Wishing to spare the generous young man further embarrassment, I returned the telephone to its cradle and quietly left the room. Sure, it was a sad moment for us, but I walked away knowing we had done the right thing.

We have become even better targets for telephone pitchmen now that NewVector Communications, a subsidiary of Ma Bell, is installing cellular mobile systems in Denver.

Instead of one antenna, the cellular system will use 10 antennas. This will improve transmission quality and will permit more people to have telephones in their automobiles.

"Congratulations, Mr. Amole! I am traveling south on the Valley Highway. It is my pleasure, sir, to inform you that you have just been named a winner of the Seam City Aluminum Corporation's Neighborhood Sweepstakes!

"Our estimated time of arrival at Bear Valley is 6:48 p.m. We will begin immediately to measure your home for our revolutionary Protecto aluminum siding. As a lucky sweepstakes winner, you will receive our estimate at absolutely no charge.

"And if you are one of the first 10 people to order this light, durable, never-needs-painting protection for your home, you will win a free opportunity to purchase a choice building site at Arid Acres, a lovely retirement community just south of Desolation, Ariz. And, Mr. Amole, if you can tell us who is buried in Grant's tomb, you will receive absolutely free . . ."

Click.

March 29, 1984

Phonophobe fear refuses to fade

CENTRAL.

Lurking somewhere in the murk that serves as my memory is that day many years ago when the telephone first came to our house. It was one of those black stand-up jobs with the earpiece suspended from the side.

A miracle! As a little kid, I would pick up the earpiece and listen in wonder as a female operator would say, "Number, pleeuz." I later learned her name was "Central."

Even though I couldn't see Central, it was my fantasy that she looked like the "It Girl," Clara Bow, a motion picture actress with whom I was infatuated. At approximately age 4, I had seen Clara Bow in the silent movie "Red Hair." I immediately fell in love with her sad eyes and her pouty, bee-stung mouth.

But my world collapsed when I saw a newspaper photograph of Clara Bow. She was clad only in step-ins and was shamelessly smoking a cigarette. How could the woman I had given my love and trust do something as patently immoral as smoke a cigarette in her step-ins?

At this point, you may choose to draw some psychological conclusions about how I have always put women on pedestals. Anyhow, it was then and there that I fell out of love with Clara Bow, Central and my telephone fantasy world. Little did I realize then, but I had become one of the first victims of an emotional ailment called "phonophobia," the fear of making phone calls.

I am relieved now to learn there are other phonophobes. I have this on no less an authority than Ava Siegler, Ph.D., a psychologist at New York University. "Many people don't do well when deprived of visual experience," Siegler writes in the October issue of Glamour magazine.

"What we depend upon in most social exchanges are non-verbal clues, such as body language and eye contact. When we are deprived of these visual clues, there's much more anxiety about anticipating a reponse and being able to control it," the article states. "On the telephone, we're reliant entirely on the auditory clues of the voice and its nuances."

I don't talk to Central anymore. She has been replaced by beeps, buzzes, tones and the voice of a female computer who is no more real than my fantasy of Clara Bow. When she comes on the line with her mechanical voice, I imagine her sitting there in her step-ins — maybe her nuances — with a cigarette hanging out of her mouth.

"Most people have trouble when they have to ask for something," Siegler believes. "They feel it puts them in an inferior position. One becomes fearful when there is a discrepancy in power — in this case, between the caller and the person called."

There sure is when I attempt to talk to the computer operator. When I ask her a simple question, she just keeps right on telling me that the number I have called is no longer in service. She accuses me of dialing in error.

"But . . . ," I start to say. She won't let me get a word in edgewise, let alone control her response. She tells me to hang up and dial again. That's when I give up. There is no way you can win a power struggle with a tape recording.

Goodbye Clara Bow, wherever you are.

September 16, 1984

Software hard sell still scary for many

ATMOPHOBIA.

How many people are there who won't use plastic bank cards? My wife, Trish, is one of them. "I refuse to use computers, and I don't trust people who do," she says with an edge of finality in her voice.

"When it comes to my money, I want to look the banker right in the eye. I also refuse to push buttons or talk to a disembodied voice at one of those drive-up windows. A bank is not a Jack-in-the-Box," she adds.

The last time she was actually in her bank was more than 20 years ago. That was when she made an auto loan to buy a Plymouth Valiant with — you guessed it — a push-button transmission. She has since done her banking by mail, and so I don't believe eye contact is the problem.

She suffers, as many do, from automated teller machine anxiety. You know the symptoms as well as I.

• Sweaty palms.
• Inability to remember personal code numbers.
• Failure to properly align magnetic strip on the card when inserting it in the slot.
• Confusion in keying in amount of cash to be withdrawn.
• Fear of leaving card in slot at conclusion of transaction.
• Dread of humiliation in front of others when the machine tells you there are insufficient funds in your account.
• Nervousness at being mugged when the machine spits out your money.

Because the bank card is playing an increasingly important role in our lives, it may be necessary to set up a therapy program for ATMophobes. The big grocery chains already have gone to an electronic check approval system requiring the card's use. No more trying to beat your short check back to the bank with a covering deposit.

In the system used at the store where I shop, the blank check goes in backward. And then the card must be put in the slide channel upside down and backward. Once you slide the card through, the computer starts beeping questions about the kind of check it is, whether it is for the amount of the groceries alone, if you want any cash back and, if so, how much.

But you have to be quick. Failure to answer the questions promptly signals the computer that you are a dodo. To punish you, the screen goes blank and makes you start over again. Because of the delay, you are held up to public ridicule simply because you have poor hand-eye coordination.

Proliferation of ATMs took another giant step recently when a savings and loan association began installing ATMs in 100 Denver-area 7-Eleven stores. This means that if you don't have enough pocket money to purchase Colorado lottery tickets while quaffing your Slurpee at the neighborhood 7-Eleven, you can get it out of your bank account from the ATM. It will be conveniently located . . . next to the Donkey Kong video game machine.

Quote: *The real danger is not that computers will begin to think like men, but that men will begin to think like computers.* — Sydney J. Harris.

December 9, 1984

Sounds of nature too precious to lose

ISOLATION.

Maui's Kaanapali Beach had been cooled by evening trade winds. There was a bronze halo around the lenticular cloud that hovered over the nearby island of Lanai. Daylight was fading and the tide whispered against the shore.

The striped sail of a single catamaran was etched on the western horizon. It moved steadily toward the harbor at Lahaina. A few gulls lazed in comfortable circles just off the reef, and their plaintive calls blended with the sound of breeze-brushed palms.

A lonely figure walked slowly through the sand, sometimes letting the insistent surf slide over her bare feet. She turned to watch the water fill her footprints. Occasionally she would pause a moment to look at the vastness of the sea, then continue her deliberate way along the deserted strip of wet sand.

I watched her until she disappeared beyond the cove. And then I looked out across the water again at the stately procession of clouds, now burnished to a deep copper by the dying sun.

There was something so sad and isolated about her. I knew she couldn't hear the tempo of the surf, the night birds in the cluster of palms, the waves as they curled to foam over the hidden coral, the distant sound of laughing children.

I knew this because she was listening to punk rock on her little Sony Walkman tape recorder.

OK, so maybe it wasn't punk rock. Perhaps it was Claude Debussy's "La Mer," Edward Elgar's "Sea Songs," or Felix Mendelssohn's "Hebrides" overture. No matter. It could have been anything. But I can't imagine a tape recording of any kind of music so beautiful as the natural sounds of that lovely evening in the islands.

Her solitary image popped into my mind because the National Fraternal Society of the Deaf is holding its 24th quadrennial convention in Denver. Some 103 delegates from the United States and Canada are meeting at the Denver Hilton Hotel to ponder the problems of those who live in silence.

If by some magic their hearing could be restored, none would take for granted songs of birds, buzz of insects, barking of dogs, crying of babies and the multitude of other sounds in our natural world.

Certainly the pocket-size tape machines are a great gift to the music lover, but I wonder sometimes about the consequences of their overuse at ear-splitting volume. Everywhere one looks, people are lost in their private worlds of recorded sound.

As my hearing fails — too many wars, too many years in a recording studio — I am increasingly conscious of the beauty of natural sound. This awareness is something like learning to walk more slowly, to take time to smell the flowers, to look at rainbows.

Hearing is precious. It shouldn't be squandered on noise, on a momentary addiction to the throb of pop music, on anything.

Quote: *How sweet the moonlight sleeps upon this bank! Here will we sit, and let the sounds of music creep in our ears: soft stillness and the night become the touches of sweet harmony.* — From "Merchant of Venice," by William Shakespeare.

July 7, 1983

On matching wits with a smart car

WHEEEP!

I don't know exactly what a decel solenoid valve does, but I have one. Same thing with my inlet manifold pressure transducer and my wastegate actuator. They are all parts of my brand new car.

Yes, I finally got new wheels. After kicking innumerable tires, fighting off platoons of salesmen and memorizing Car and Driver, I bought a 1984 three-door, cherry-red Saab 900 APC Turbo, manufactured at Trollhatten, Sweden. Yumpin' Yimminy! That little sucker can really move!

I bought it at Deane Buick-Saab from Rich Osner, a special accounts representative. That must mean he is a salesman. Actually, I sold myself on the car during the years I did radio commercials about the Saab for Dick Deane on KVOD. The easiest person to sell is another salesperson. I have always been a sucker for my own pitches.

I went to sleep the other night while trying to wade through my Vehicle Owner's Manual. I awakened at midnight after dreaming I had to take a test on its contents.

In my nightmare, I had flunked because I couldn't explain the function of the Lambda Control System. "You dummy!" Osner was shouting at me in my dream. "The Lambda Control System is a closed loop feedback adapted to the CI to constantly maintain close air/fuel ratio control under all operating conditions. Go back and study your manual until you get it right!"

The Saab people describe the 900 as "the most intelligent automobile ever built," prompting me to wonder if I might be overmatched with such a smart car. I seem to be doing reasonably well, though. Maybe there is an electronic sensor that tells the Saab when there is a boob at the wheel, and it somehow compensates.

I have had some trouble accommodating myself to the ThefTrap auto alarm. It is supposed to foil crooks who try to steal your car or rip off the stereo. I'll have to say one thing; it sure scares the pants off me. It emits an ear-splitting "Wheeep! Wheeep! Wheeep!" if you are not careful how you get in and out of the car.

Unless you turn on the ignition with the key within 15 seconds after unlocking the car, ThefTrap starts wheeeping like crazy. I holler back at the thing, "Hey, I'm not the the thief, I am the owner!" But it goes right on wheeeping until I turn the key.

I tried to explain this to my dog, Yazzie, when I was draining him in the park the other night. I told him to jump into the car just as soon as I unlocked the door. But just as I did, old Yazzie decided to take one more squirt at a willow tree.

"Wheeep! Wheeep! Wheeep!" shrieked ThefTrap. Poor old Yazzie didn't know what to do. The old VW never wheeeped at him. Frightened, he skittered into the bushes.

There I was, trying to decide whether to run after old Yazzie, or fumble around and find the ignition key to turn off the wheeeping. I have encountered the same problem getting my wife into the car, even though she doesn't skitter into the bushes. There just isn't time to unlock the passenger side, run around to the driver's side, get in and disarm ThefTrap before it wheeeps.

I suppose I'll get the hang of it.

June 28, 1984

Artificial hearts vs. real starvation

ANDROIDS.

Salt Lake City doctors are looking for another Barney Clark. Now that the U.S. Food and Drug Administration has approved new guidelines for artificial-heart implants, the University of Utah Medi-cal Center is ready to go.

Clark, the world's first artificial-heart recipient, died March 28, 1983, 112 days after being hooked up to a 375-pound compressed-air drive unit. He was never well enough to leave the hospital.

Being one who believes that the quality of life is at least as important as its length, I was not impressed when we were told it was not Clark's polyurethane ticker that failed, but his other organs. What a wonderful medical victory! How sad that Clark was not alive to join in the celebration.

"We are now in the process of finding a patient for the next clinical (implantation) of an artificial heart," said Dr. William C. DeVries, the only physician authorized by the FDA to do such surgery.

Dr. Richard Lee, heart team coordinator, wouldn't speculate on how long it would take to locate one. It took nine months for physicians to find Clark.

The new FDA guidelines permit doctors at the medical center to select a healthier candidate than Clark. DeVries said the second implant could take place "within the next day, if possible. . . . We are ready right now. At this moment." He said he is screening candidates "who have healthy bodies but very sick hearts."

In our never-ending pursuit of mechanical immortality, the list of artificial spare parts continues to grow. Is it beyond reason that we can phase out human equipment entirely and let androids take over?

The clearance for another artificial-heart implant comes at a time when we are involved in heavy debate on how long life should be prolonged artificially. At great cost, heroic means can keep organs alive long after the brain ceases to function.

In the cloudy background of all of this is an engineering compulsion to create equipment just because it is possible. It isn't often that consequences of technology are considered before the technology is created. We worry about that later.

The irony is that we invest huge sums of money and great intellectual resources to lengthen the life of someone who has a healthy body and a sick heart, but we do little to save the lives of millions who die from starvation and from disease we can successfully treat.

I am offended by that contradiction. It isn't that I am opposed to medical research. It is more that the development of the artifical heart may be premature when measured against more urgent medical needs.

Somewhere along the line we must come to accept human frailty. We are not supposed to live forever. Like it or not, nature supplies the means to control our population.

Our reverence for life is carried beyond the extreme when we turn on our television to watch a poor old guy hooked up to a machine, gasping his life away. This is not a medical triumph. It is a personal indignity and a crime against nature.

June 21, 1984

Life's becoming oversimplification

SIMPLIFICATION.

The Idea Fairy was pulling off her mittens when I came into the newsroom. There were a few flakes of unmelted snow in her hair. I could tell by the stack of tiny parcels on my desk that she had been Christmas shopping.

ME — Have you been doing your patriotic duty by spending money?

FAIRY — Don't be cynical. What's wrong with helping the economy grow out of the deficit by buying a few Christmas presents?

ME — Nothing, so long as you are not reducing the national debt by increasing your personal debt. And besides, I thought it was tax simplification that was going to cut the deficit.

FAIRY — Were you born under a cabbage leaf, Buster? "Tax simplification" has replaced "revenue enhancement" as the euphemism for tax increase.

ME — But President Reagan told us taxes would be increased over his dead body.

FAIRY — We can't wait that long. Congress won't cut social programs. Reagan won't cut defense spending. I only hope they don't cut back on space exploration.

ME — The shuttle program has become so routine they are going to take along a schoolteacher and a Republican senator.

FAIRY — Would you like to be the first columnist in space?

ME — I have taken myself out of contention should NASA ever get that low on the passenger pecking order.

FAIRY — Really? What an adventure! Everyone wants to travel in space.

ME — Not this old kid. I'm not going until they get the toilet working better. I can't imagine anything worse than drifting around Earth in orbit with a stopped up biffy. When you are 330 miles in space and the plumbing goes bad, you can't just run down to the neighborhood Conoco station.

FAIRY — Oh, Buster! When are you ever going to elevate your thinking above the bathroom level? Where is your imagination? Where is your scientific curiosity? Just think, they are actually putting mechanical hearts in human beings.

ME — You can take me out of contention for plastic hearts, too. When my heart gives out, I'll do my duty to Governor Lamm and die.

FAIRY — You say that now. But how will you feel when the time comes?

ME — I'll remember Barney Clark's last 112 days. When he did die, the plastic heart "kept on ticking," as John Cameron Swayze used to say when he removed a Timex wristwatch from the motorboat propeller on TV. If that's immortality, you can have it.

FAIRY — It wasn't Clark's artificial heart that went bad. It was his liver.

ME — That's the way it is these days. Doctors always blame death on something else. When I was a kid, if a doctor was treating you for something, by golly, that's what you died of, not something else.

FAIRY — That was then. Now is now.

ME — I suppose. We owe a lot to progress. Take the deregulation of the phone company and the airlines, for instance.

FAIRY — I can see this conversation is going no further.

ME — Right. We're out of space.

November 27, 1984

8

ALL IN THE FAMILY

Trish in two roles

TRISH.

My wife. It is time you knew her better. She is blond, quite young and attractive and a woman who is caught in the middle.

She has had both career and family. And for quite a few of the 14 years we have been married, she filled both roles at the same time.

Trish worked regularly as a registered nurse until about one year ago. I can remember when she decided to quit. I knew it was coming by the way she looked when she got home after midnight. I would come downstairs and find her sitting in the kitchen. She would be sort of looking at the table.

It wasn't just caring for the terminal patients that burned her out, it also was trying to deal with their distraught families. There was something else. There never seemed to be enough nurses. As health care costs have increased, the RNs have been spread thinner and thinner.

It is bad enough that nurses are overworked and underpaid. What is sometimes even worse is the way they feel about what they do. They come home after work feeling guilty because they didn't have enough time to give proper patient care.

But that's all behind Trish now. She is out of it. I am happy for her, although a bit sorry her skills have been lost to her profession.

She has always managed to keep her sharp sense of humor through all of this. That really was to have been the point of this column when I started writing it.

I thought about this the other night while we were attending a delightful little party in the home of a friend of mine. There were a lot of career women there. Most of them were young and married, but had kept their maiden names. The conversation was witty and intelligent.

Trish Amole is shy and feels unnecessarily intimidated in these situations. She just sat there and said nothing as the conversation went: "Buzz, buzz, buzz Dick Lamm. Buzz, buzz, buzz the Denver Symphony Orchestra. Buzz, buzz, buzz Marvin Davis."

There was more buzzing. Finally, there was a little moment of silence. The others looked over at Trish. With only the slightest hesitation, she smiled, raised one finger and said, "I baked two dozen chocolate-chip cookies yesterday."

A lot of her off-the-wall humor is based on fantasy. She assumes other identities when it suits her mood. It happened the other night while just the two of us were having a quiet dinner at a small Castle Rock restaurant.

Trish looked up from her salad and said, "Listen, after we leave here, why don't we go back to my condominium and you could spend the night. OK?"

"That would be nice," I said, pretending we weren't married and didn't live in Bear Valley.

"Oh, I'm so glad you'll be able to stay over," she said.

"Why?"

"Because I already made the bran muffins."

She gives other people identities she feels they ought to have. We were in Dave Cook's not long ago when she spotted a young, bearded man. He was buying a basketball.

"He's a dental student," Trish said flatly. "He lives in a small apartment in the University Park area. He has lots of books and there are plants in the window."

"You don't know that," I said.

"Yes I do. He is a senior and is buying the basketball so he can stay in shape," she whispered. "The exercise will do him good. Help him unwind when he takes his state boards. There's a basketball hoop over the garage door, in the driveway at the back of the apartment."

Trish probably will be upset when she reads this. If she is, I'll deny writing it. I'll blame it on the guy with the basketball. In addition to having a fair hook shot, I am told he writes an occasional newspaper column.

July 25, 1979

Domicile invaded by 'administrator'

UPSCALE.

My wife, Trish, is fed up with being housewife and mother. She has decided to change her job classification to "Domicile Systems Administrator."

Susan and I knew something was up by the way she fixed up the den. It is no longer a tacky little place to take a nap on Sunday afternoon. It is now the Office of the Administrator.

You ought to see it. On the uncluttered desk is a telephone, coffee mug filled with freshly sharpened pencils, a legal-size yellow pad, high-intensity lamp, alphabetized telephone listings and a double-deck wire "in" and "out" basket.

Beside the desk is a typewriter and stand. There are bookcases, maps on the wall and a couple of accordion letter files. The big metal filing cabinet comes next week.

Trish can't wait for that. She has file folders ready. They are the kind with the colored index tabs. "I have broken down the household duties into different categories," she explained. "The file marked red is for the bedroom, or 'Sleeping System Facility,' as we will now call it.

"Yellow is for the kitchen, or 'Food Preparation Central.' I haven't decided whether to use the green file for the bathroom, or 'Personal Sanitation Facility,' or maybe for the utility room, or 'Laundry and Clothing Maintenance,' as we shall henceforth refer to it."

My wife is an office supply junkie. She has been squirreling away paper clips, gummed reinforcements, spiral notebooks, outliner markers, graph paper, manila folders, ring binders and brown envelopes for years.

Now, I guess she has decided to make her move.

She seemed annoyed the other day when I complained that socks in my drawer didn't match. "Did you have an appointment to see the administrator?" she said evenly.

"My socks don't match."

"It will be necessary for you to file a 'Laundry and Clothing Maintenance Discrepancy Form.' Include in it the time and date of apparel loss, a description of the missing article, estimated value of said item, and also a narrative explanation, not exceeding 50 words, of your negligence."

"My sock . . ."

"Your sock, as you call it, is your responsibility, Mr. Amole. I am the administrator. It is not my function to maintain catalog control over your personal belongings. This interview is terminated."

With that, Trish turned on her heel and disappeared into her office.

It has been like that for several days now. Susan isn't crazy about the new setup either. She got caught sneaking a Pepsi out of the refrigerator. "Susan," the administrator said, "that container — soft drink, carbonated — was not properly requisitioned from 'Central Supply.' Return it to inventory immediately."

There's more, of course. But I can't take time now to go into it. I have to get cracking on my "Torn T-Shirt Control Summary." Susan is working on her "Shampoo Spillage Declaration." And Trish?

In her office, I suppose.

June 17, 1982

He's all washed up

LEFTOVERS.

The Idea Fairy was perched on the corner of my Associated Press Stylebook and Libel Manual when I walked into the newsroom.

IDEA FAIRY — How's it going, Big Guy?

ME — What is this "big guy" business?

IDEA FAIRY — Oh, nothing. Just trying to reinforce the macho in you. Do you smell something funny? Sort of like apricots?

ME — It's my hair.

FAIRY — Your hair?

ME — Yes. I washed my hair this morning with Earth Born Natural pH Non-Alkaline Apricot Essence Shampoo.

FAIRY — You want to talk about it, Big Guy?

ME — I do not require any macho reinforcement. Being the only male in our house, I have to use up all the leftover shampoo.

FAIRY — Is that a problem?

ME — My wife and daughter never finish a bottle of shampoo. They flit from one brand to the next in never-ending pursuit of shinier, bouncier hair with more body. I am too frugal to see the leftovers go to waste.

FAIRY — So that's why you smell like apricots.

ME — Only until next week. I am about to tackle a half-bottle of Lemongrass Concentrated Golden Lotus. I don't know whether my hair will smell like lemongrass, whatever that is, or lotus.

FAIRY — After that?

ME — There's a part-bottle of Jheri Redding Milk 'n Honee Salon Formula Protein Shampoo in the shower. And then I'll splash on some Revlon FLEX Balsam and Protein Creme Rinse and Conditioner with tangle control plus shine you can see!

FAIRY — The only thing about you that shines, Buster, is the top of your head.

ME — No point in being nasty, Shorty.

FAIRY — I was kidding. But do you make it your business to dispose of all the leftovers at your house?

ME — That's not all bad. I love leftover pot roast sandwiches. Beef stew improves overnight. I wear some of my sons' old clothes left in the basement when they moved away. Waste not, want not.

FAIRY — Admirable. You are concerned about what is called the disposable society?

ME — Sure, but there is more to it than that. Every now and then I pick up a real collectors' item.

FAIRY — Like what?

ME — I have a Denver Country Club towel in absolutely mint condition.

FAIRY — You stole it?

ME — Of course not. I don't know how we got it. Like our cat, it just sort of came to our house one day.

FAIRY — Are you going to return it?

ME — You're kidding. The place intimidates me. The only time I go over there is to have lunch with Bob Knous. Besides, I like the towel. It is classy.

FAIRY — You are fantasizing with the towel?

ME — Not really. I have a Holiday Inn towel, and one I prize very highly from the old Hayward Hotel in Los Angeles. But I am really very fond of the Denver Country Club towel.

FAIRY — I can't believe you are saying this.

ME — It would be nice to have a towel from Cherry Hills Country Club. In the pecking order of country clubs, Cherry Hills is just a shade under the Denver Country Club.

FAIRY — Buster!

ME — And then maybe one from Lakewood Country Club.

FAIRY — You are an elitist, a class-conscious elitist.

ME — No. I'm just out of towels.

October 27, 1981

Reflections on a bald spot

SKINHEAD.

There I was in a hotel bathroom with mirrors on all four walls. Ever have that happen? You get to see more of yourself than God ever intended. Doesn't matter which way you turn, you see front, back and both sides.

Few of us are so attractive or so narcissistic we need floor-to-ceiling mirrors fore and aft. That bathroom was decorated in what might be described as Early Hugh Hefner, or perhaps Playboy Quatorze. Whatever it was, it wasn't for this old boy.

My problem with all those mirrors was that I couldn't shave without seeing the back of my head. I didn't need to be reminded of MPB, male pattern baldness.

I have almost decided to write my next book on the subject. The title will be "Skinhead Strategies." It will come in a plain brown wrapper and will be sold through the mail. No red-blooded male wants to look like James Watt or Sen. Alan Cranston.

MPB is irreversible. There are only two medical solutions: transplants and scalp reduction. The latter is a relatively new technique in which a surgeon cuts out the bald spot and stitches the hairy fringes together. It is sort of like a face lift. The danger, of course, is that when all the tucks are made and the skin has tightened, you might turn out looking wide-eyed, innocent and perpetually smiling like Nancy Reagan.

There are some non-medical things MPB victims can do. If you are Jewish and spiritually inclined, you can wear a yarmulke at all times to cover your bald spot. Christians have the option of joining a monastery where the style is to have the crown of the head shaved, bald or not.

If there isn't enough hair to comb over the bald spot, shave off the rest. Only two people out of the millions who have tried this have made it work: Yul Brynner and Telly Savalas. But what the heck, maybe you'll be No. 3. Nothing ventured, nothing gained.

For those who have a few mansard wisps remaining in front, giving the illusion of hair, there is the clever footwork gambit that bears my name. I perfected the Amole Clever Footwork Gambit while watching cutting horses at the National Western Stock Show, Horse Show and Rodeo.

They are marvelous animals. By constantly facing the cattle, the horses anticipate every move. They keep working the critters until they are herded into the corner of the corral. The main thing the horse does is always to face the cattle and never let even one of them get behind him.

I do that at cocktail parties. I try to be the last one to arrive. Then I start working the other guests in much the same fashion as the cutting horse controls the cattle. I dart from one side of the room to the other, always keeping everyone in front of me.

By being subtly aggressive, I am able to drive all the guests into the corner of the rumpus room. Once they are all crowded together, I thank the hostess and smilingly back from the room through the front door. Once outside, I disappear into the shadows and no one has seen my MPB.

Quote: *My hair has prematurely turned to skin.* — Carl Akers.

August 19, 1984

He wants to deal on an automobile

WHEELS.

"Before you leave this lot, I'm gonna talk to management," the car salesman said. "We wanna put you behind the steering wheel of a new 1984 Chrysler Laser turbo. We wanna make you a Bill Crouch customer."

That's about the way it went Saturday as I hacked my way through the underbrush of "Sell-A-Thons," "Deal-A-Thons" and even a "Help-A-Thon." I'm shopping for a new car, and I don't mind telling you it's a pain in the old rusty dusty.

My daughter, Susan, is about to take over my '79 VW Rabbit, and I need some new wheels. I have purchased five VWs since Carl Akers talked me out of my Corvette and into something sensible.

That Corvette was some kind of bad machine. One time in Idaho, I opened everything but the tool box. By the time I lost my nerve, telephone poles looked like a fine-toothed comb and everything else was a blur.

Most of the cars I have had since have been company cars. Now that I no longer have a company, I have to deal with the wide and wonderful world of retail automobile sales on my own.

My wife, Trish, thinks I should upscale into something classy. "Not too nice, though," she advised. "People will think you are the chauffeur and tell you how lucky you are to have a job driving a car like that."

The family consensus is that I should buy something youthful; a car with some pizazz. I don't know, though. Those Z babies fancied by the young hunks who hang around fern bars wouldn't make me any younger.

That's pretty much a lost cause. I had hoped the Denver Free University would have a course this summer entitled "Break Dancing for Seniors," but there was nothing like that in the catalog.

In my weekend auto odyssey, I was pleasantly surprised to find that "Papa" Joe Luby is still alive, well and doing business in Lakewood. He is certainly one of the last of the old-time car dealers. Papa is a survivor.

I remember when his Chevy agency was down at 14th and Larimer. That was before Dana Crawford even imagined Larimer Square. Papa was around when there was a Stovall and a Hilliker, a Murphy and a Mahoney, a Swayne and a Wimbush and a Hoskins and a Beatty. Dealer franchises in those days were handed carefully and lovingly from one generation to the next, not passed around like a plate of stale cookies.

"I still drive a Corvette," the white-haired Papa confided. "As I get older, I find getting in the thing is not much more difficult than it used to be. It's the getting out that's tougher."

Papa didn't pressure me. He sort of let me sniff around and kick some tires. I appreciated that. Moments like those in a car agency are rare in these times of push and shove.

I have no idea what I'll wind up buying. I don't know a CRX from an RX-7 GSL. I kind of like the 318i and the 2M4, but the 4000S and the awesome 300 ZX are nice, too. The 190E 2.3 looks awfully expensive, but they say the new 318s will blow 'em in the weeds. I may have to settle for something practical like the 505S or the GL.

Maybe I'll just get another VW.

June 5, 1984

Cords and jeans don't meet codes

DRESS CODE.

On those rare occasions when Trish and I go out at night, my apparel is a subject for domestic debate.

"What are you going to wear?" I ask as I sit on the edge of the bed in my undershorts.

"Just any old thing," she replies. "Why?"

"Well, I just thought maybe I ought to have some idea. I don't want to get all dressed up if I don't have to."

"I'm just going to wear something I can knock around in. We're supposed to come casual. You should be able to figure that out. You're old enough to dress yourself."

With that, I slip into a fresh pair of jeans, clean tube socks and a nice, soft, old cotton shirt. It doesn't take me long to get ready, so I start down the stairs to go watch TV until Trish gets ready.

"You're not going to wear that?" a voice behind me says.

"You said it was casual. What you see before you is the casual Gene Amole."

"I said casual, not tacky. I won't go out with you like that. If we go up to the house and you are dressed the way you are, they'll send you around to the back door."

I look up at Trish, and she is standing there in a rust linen skirt and a beige silk blouse with a gold pendant on a neck chain.

"I thought you said this was casual? Look at you. I don't call that casual. Is Marvin Davis going to be there?"

Knowing I have to upscale, I go back to the bedroom closet and start rummaging through my limited wardrobe.

"Don't go overboard," Trish warns from the other room.

Fortunately, there's a pair of corduroys just back from the cleaners. I put them on with my genuine imitation alligator belt and a knit shirt with a little penguin on the pocket. I start down the stairs again.

"Penguins are square. You look like you're going to a 1950s sock hop. And besides, those corduroys whistle when you walk."

Trish has changed into a little Geoffrey Beene number. It is a black-and-ivory pinstripe jacket that reverses to a floral printed wool challis, silk matelasse blouse and dirndl skirt. I know when I'm whipped. It's back to the closet.

This time I come up with a pair of fawn-colored slacks, brown loafers, floral sport shirt — open at the collar — and one of my daughter's gold neck chains.

"We are not going to a fern bar," Trish says icily. She is now dressed in a Charles Kleibacker silk, gold-lighted chiffon gown in pearl gray. She is wearing a green and lavender jade necklace and bracelet to match.

I trudge back to the bedroom and put on my gray slacks, white button-down shirt with old school tie and my blue blazer.

"You can get by in that," she says grudgingly.

When we finally get to the party, I note Trish has changed into a tuxedo outfit with light wool morning jacket, silk blouse and hip-yoked skirt. We go inside.

You guessed it. The guys are all sitting around in jeans, corduroys and knit shirts with little penguins on the pocket.

July 1, 1982

Upwardly mobile? No, just mobile

RUNNER.

In her relentless compulsion to upgrade my appearance, Trish has been trying to get me to wear trendy shoes. Wives are like that. They believe the contents of a book can be improved by changing its cover.

But I've not had much luck. Not the Gucci type, I guess. Same thing for all the other expensive "kicks," as we used to call shoes. I paid 90 bucks for a pair of French Shriner loafers that are absolute torture.

That's the problem with buying most shoes. How can you tell whether new shoes will be comfortable until they are broken in? Buying shoes is like getting married or purchasing a used car. You don't know what you have until it is too late to take it back.

Getting the right size is my problem. Each time a clerk hunkers over my feet with one of those foot-measuring gizmos, I can hear in my memory Fats Waller's raspy voice:

Up in Harlem at a table for two/there wuz four of us: me, your big feet and you./From your ankles up you sure are sweet/but from there on down they's just too much feet./Your feets too big./Don't want you 'cause your feets too big./Can't use you 'cause your feets too big./I really hates you 'cause your feets too big.

But I have found my own personal solution to the shoe-fit dilemma. For some strange reason I get a perfect fit with Kinney shoes. When I asked Trish to explain this, she said, "You have cheap feet."

I make no secret of my preference for Kinney shoes. Wouldn't do any good. Every time I walk through a puddle of water, I leave behind the telltale footprint of the company slogan: "GASS, GASS, GASS, GASS." It is stamped on the bottom of the rubber soles and it means "Great American Shoe Store."

As a designer label, I don't suppose it ranks up there with ESPRIT, Calvin Klein or Polo, but I'll give up a lot of prestige for just a small amount of comfort. And comfort is what I get from my new Kinney Stadia running shoes.

Running shoes?

Oh, of course I don't run. You know better than that. I am one of those who walks . . . and slowly. But I have noted lately it has become sartorially acceptable to come to work in running shoes. You see them worn with three-piece suits, blazers and slacks as well as other business attire. It has a lot to do with the fitness rage.

On-the-make junior executives are expected to become sweating thinclads during the noon hour as they huff and puff through our downtown carbon monoxide. We are all supposed to make way for them in the interest of public health and their desire for corporate status.

And so if you see me downtown in my running shoes, understand I am wearing them not to be upwardly mobile. Slow and deliberate horizontal mobility is my game.

I suppose I run the risk of being mistaken at some distance for a junior executive, but not, certainly, from the ankles up. That's just a chance I'll have to take.

Quote: *I base most of my fashion taste on what doesn't itch.* — Gilda Radner.

April 24, 1984

The clothesmule

MISTAKEN IDENTITY.

I have one of those faces that blends in with the crowd. People are always confusing me with someone else. A lady once stopped me on the street and insisted that I was taller when I worked at Colorado National Bank.

I tried to explain that I never had worked at Colorado National Bank and that I was never any taller than I was at that moment. She wouldn't believe it. I don't know how many times I have heard people whisper: "There goes old what's-his-name."

It happened again the other day, only this time it was my career identity that was confused. I came away from the incident convinced that something must be done to upgrade my appearance.

I had just parked my car in the Allright lot at West 14th Avenue and Elati Street. It is one of those places where you park your own car and put money in a slot. A woman turned in from the street in a little foreign car. She stopped, rolled down her window and said, "Is there room to park here?"

It didn't take long for the message to sink in. "She thinks I am the parking lot attendant," I said to myself.

"Madame, is it your impression that I am a parking lot attendant?"

"Well, aren't you?"

"I neither park cars, nor do I do windows," I snapped. "Furthermore, I do not speak to strange women on the streets."

Actually, I didn't snap anything. What I did do was mumble that I was sorry I wasn't the attendant. I helped her park her car and showed her where to put her money. As I walked across the street to the Rocky Mountain News building, I began to come up with the clever rejoinders. It has always been that way with me. Give me enough time and I'll top anyone.

Why did she think I was the parking lot attendant? Body language? No, it must have been the way I was dressed. Nothing wrong with floppy corduroy pants, sweater, old Pendleton jacket and wool cap. Not a thread of polyester on my body. If it weren't for the white tube socks, I would have looked almost preppie. That is, if a man in his late 50s can look preppie.

Maybe it was the cap. It is an Irish one. Not exactly in the highest of style, I suppose. George Kane, our entertainment editor, is fond of saying to me: "Hi, Sluggo. Where's Nancy?"

We are not exactly slaves to fashion at the News, except maybe for the business section people. They spiff up, probably because they have to deal with the big hummers of our town. The rest of us have adopted what feature writer John Ashton once called "the elegant but funky look."

It varies from person to person, but among the males it usually involves a shirt and tie, sport jacket, faded jeans and jogging shoes.

Still, I can't recall that anyone else around here ever has been mistaken for a parking lot attendant. Bill Gallo parks at the same place I do. No one ever says to him: "I'll be back in two hours. Don't nick the doors."

I used to try to dress the way I thought a columnist ought to dress — dark suit, felt hat, tie loosened at the neck. Didn't work. People in the newsroom made sport of me. Somehow, I came off more as an unemployed storm window salesman. For some people, clothes make the man. In my case, it appears more that the man made the clothes.

Quote: *Trust not the heart of that man to whom old clothes are not venerable.* — Thomas Carlyle.

March 22, 1981

Privacy invasion medicine enough

I'M HERE.

The quickest way to get me back on the job after suffering a case of the dread mopus is to put a little note in the newspaper that says: "No Amole Column. Gene Amole is ill. His column will resume soon."

Soon is now. I don't know why it is necessary to invade my privacy by telling the whole world I have the trots. When my pal Suzy Weiss is home with the sniffles, we don't put an item in the newspaper that says: "Suzanne Weiss is ill. Her coverage of City Hall news will resume soon."

It upsets my mother when she reads in the newspaper that I am sick. There is one thing I learned long ago about the column-writing game: Even if no one else reads your stuff, your mother will. My mother harbors the illusion that her 61-year-old son is still a little boy and is unable to take care of himself. She worries.

Other family members are not similarly concerned, however. "Someone at school said you're sick," my daughter said in that detatched way of hers. "You don't look sick to me."

My wife, the registered nurse, made chicken soup. She warned me again, as she has in the past, "Look, if you are really sick, for heaven's sake, don't let them send you to the hospital."

Small chance of that. There is very little of my original equipment remaining to treat, remove or repair. There was a time when I was addicted to hospitals. It all started back in 1956 when I had a subtotal gastric resection (a hunk of my stomach was removed). "Congratulations, Mr. Amole!" the recovery room nurse gushed. "You have just broken the AAU record for the number of bleeding ulcers."

Tonsils, appendix, hernia repairs, knee, eye and back surgery — I have had them all. How I glow with pride when I think of all the physicians and their lovely families I have packed off on fun-filled, sun-filled vacations in the Caribbean. Fortunately, I ran out of diseased organs and broken cartilage just before I ran out of money.

I have managed to hang onto my gallbladder, however. I intend to keep it as a memento of what I used to be. When my time comes and I go to the great newsroom in the sky, old cronies will gather outside the undertaking parlor after the service, and someone will brush away a final tear and say, "Good old Geno. Gallbladder was sound as a dollar."

It used to be tough getting in a hospital. You needed reservations. Not anymore. There is intense competition among hospitals for patients now that there are so many empty beds. They are promoting and advertising as though they were discount furniture stores. There are special wards for female-related problems, cardiac patients, alcoholism treatment and other medical specialties.

The next thing, I suppose, will be to offer premiums the way savings-and-loan associations once did. An appendectomy ought to be worth at least an electric toaster. Hemorrhoid removal will get you a clock radio at least. What would they give you for a case of the trots?

Kaopectate, probably.

March 3, 1985

You are falling asleep, you are . . .

DEVIATED.

Being a longtime insomniac, I was interested in that article Sunday by Pam Avery, our award-winning Rocky Mountain News medical writer. It was about sleep disorders and treatment strategies available.

It all began for me years ago when my nose and upper lip were ripped open by a strand of barbed wire. The man who stitched me back together did a reasonable job in restoring my appearance, but he left me with a deviated septum.

When I try to sleep, my nostrils clog, I breathe through my mouth, the tongue goes dry, and I wake up. Corrective surgery is available, but I have avoided it.

I was told while I was still in broadcasting that my deviated septum enhanced my radio voice. Don't have the operation, I was advised, or my career as an announcer will end.

I can recall a strange dream I had at the time. In it, I was listening to an old Atwater-Kent radio. A familiar voice was saying: "Good evening, ladies and gentlemen. From high atop the beautiful Hotel Riffraff, overlooking glittering downtown Chama, New Mexico, it's the toe-tapping music of Gene Amole, his deviated septum and his orchestra."

My insomnia problems are more than physical. I am one of those who can't turn off his mind. When it's time to snooze, I begin to tackle all the problems of the world. You wouldn't believe the creative solutions I have found for strife in Central America, high interest rates, the Lowry landfill and even the heartbreak of psoriasis.

But I can never remember the details in the morning. I tried keeping a pad and pencil by the bed. But my scrawl turned out to be nothing more than "Fistaris the kranastan, and schmiggle it now!"

At the Presbyterian Hospital sleep disorders center, patients are advised not to take naps but to go out and get some fresh air. Lordy! If it weren't for naps, I wouldn't get any sleep at all. I can sleep anywhere, anytime I am not supposed to. I have had some of my best sleep while attending sessions of the Colorado Legislature.

I will nod off instantly at the very mention of the Upper Colorado River Compact Commission. There is nothing so dull as water law. When a man wearing steel-rim glasses stands up beside a Bureau of Reclamation contour map and begins to point out aquifers, my eyes glaze and I am gone.

Why is it that our deepest and most relaxing sleep comes just as we are supposed to wake up? You can battle the pillows and blankets all night, but five minutes before the alarm is supposed to ring, you at last fall into a wonderful slumber.

What we need are sandmen (sandwomen, sandpersons). It is such a wonderful gift some have for putting others to sleep. In my case, I would pay well to have a member of the board of directors of the Regional Transportation District come out to my house at beddytime.

He would give me some sugar cookies and milk, tuck me in and then tell me a story about a fixed-guideway transit system. ZZZZZZZZZZ.

May 15, 1984

If at first you fail — it's too late

MISTAKES.

Do you ever wonder who is really in charge of the family? Is it the parents or their kids? One thing is sure: few of us are sufficiently mature to become parents before the kids actually arrive.

"The value of marriage," wrote Peter de Vries, "is not that adults produce children but that children produce adults." There is no suitable training for life's most important work. And the worst of it is that by the time parents realize what mistakes they have made, it is too late to do much about correcting them.

Sigmund Freud was onto something when he described the first six years of life as formative years. Parental mistakes in nurturing can sometimes produce irreversible consequences.

In most cases, the best-intentioned of parents really don't understand this. They act out their roles as fathers or mothers in much the same way their parents did. "Like father, like son," as the old saw goes.

I think about this every Father's Day. Looking back as far as I can in my life, I don't really know how I could have turned out to be any other kind of person. Although there were certainly major personality differences between my father and my grandfather, and my father and me, we were remarkably alike in important ways.

Although we shared some significant strengths, we also shared plenty of weaknesses. Not the least of these was a common inability to be open with our families. We guarded our feelings in much the same way a hungry man protects a last crust of bread.

I don't know why. Grandpa had an explosive temper. Pop could also blow his cork. And I have had to face the fact that there is plenty of fury behind my folksy facade.

Although we were good at expressing anger, we threw up the barricades when it came to revealing private feelings of tenderness, frustration, disappointment, fear, love, pain, jealousy and anxiety.

It is more comfortable to write of these things than to speak of them. I suppose I have deluded myself into thinking that I am really writing about someone else. That's not me up there in print. It is some other poor boob.

How this stoic Amole behavior began I don't know. Its genesis is hidden somewhere in our family's murky past. This business of denying our humanity has rippled from one generation to the next.

I suppose if I had recognized this as a younger man, I might consciously have been more open to my children and would have been a better father. It is difficult, however, to straighten the branch once the twig has been bent.

The Father's Day message in all of this is not just for dads. It is for parents in general. We must somehow come to learn how critically important those formative years are.

We must be sensitive to our special responsibilities during that time. We must not be afraid to let our children know we have feelings that are honest and human and that we do have weaknesses.

Not easy, is it?

June 17, 1984

Aloha, non-person

STRANGER IN PARADISE.

After an exciting tour of Hawaiian dress shops, Trish, Susan and I were finally on the tropical paradise island of Maui, named after the magnificent demigod.

Legend has it that he created the Hawaiian islands when his fishhook caught the ocean's bottom. He then snared the sun and forced it to slow its passage over the islands, allowing Hawaiians more time to fish.

They talk that way a lot over there. Hawaiian people are noted for their ability to make up an appropriate legend on the spot, so long as there are two tourists willing to listen.

Not being much of a sun worshiper, I did have some pleasant times walking Maui's lovely beaches at dawn and dusk. I don't know how people get anything done over there. I never tire of watching and listening to the surf.

It was on one of these beach sorties near the town of Lahaina that I booked us on the Scotch Mist for an afternoon sail, whale watch and snorkle expedition.

The other passengers included a Canadian couple. They let it be known immediately that they were certified divers. The sixth passenger was a bikini-clad woman. She identified herself as the operator of Maui's only tattoo parlor.

There was an interesting floral design on her right thigh. It made its way up and around her leg, disappearing under the bottom half of her bikini. I won't speculate on where the design terminated or what it did when it got there. The skipper was a tall, bronzed man by the name of Doug. He had a female associate. She wore a tight lavender bathing suit and was some punkins.

Things went well enough as we sailed out from Lahaina. The idea was to anchor and snorkle over the coral reefs to examine a variety of exotic tropical fish. Duck soup for the Canadians. They slipped easily into the water and paddled out across the bay. Although she had never snorkled before, Susan needed only a few minutes before she was popping in and out of the water like a porpoise. Trish had the good judgment to remain on the boat.

I don't recall whether I jumped, was pushed or fell into the water. I can only remember that at the moment of splash, my flippers came off and I lost my mask and breathing apparatus. Doug threw me a rope and a life preserver. Susan managed to rescue my flippers and mask. Once they hauled me back on board, Doug looked at me and said, "I don't think I want you to go back in the water. Ever."

Once Susan, the Canadians and the tattoo lady were back on board, we set sail again. Out to the open sea. There was a stiff afternoon wind. The Scotch Mist knifed through the waves. The sails were snapping as Doug skillfully tacked the trim little sloop through the spray.

The Canadians were speaking of diving off the coast of Cozumel. The tattoo lady and Doug's associate were forward, laughing over some private matter. Trish and Susan were thoroughly enjoying their first sailing adventure. I had moved to the stern of the craft. Salty fluids from my gastrointestinal plumbing were making their way into my mouth. I knew I was going to be sick.

"My God, look at that whale!" the tattoo lady shouted.

"Biggest sucker I ever saw," Doug hollered.

"He came completely out of the water," someone else added.

I didn't see the whale. My head was hanging over the back of the boat and I was pitching my cookies into the Pacific. It was that way until we got back to Lahaina. I gagged and heaved and choked. I managed to look up once, and everyone was still having a marvelous time. I had been declared a non-person and deserved it.

Aloha.

April 28, 1981

Requiem for a cat who loved tales

CAT.

He never had a fancy name as some cats do. We started calling him "CAT," with capital letters, because that's what it said on his rabies tag. Over at Anderson Animal Hospital, I think he is listed on their records as "Mr. CAT." Sometimes we called him "Kitty."

It was at least 10 years ago he turned up at our front door on a cold, windy night. CAT always hated wind. Trish and Susan gave him some milk, and he stayed on.

Oh, I was against it. Never had much truck with cats. They made my skin itch and my eyes water. And besides, I didn't think taking on a cat was fair to our dog, Yazzie.

But I was outnumbered. Gradually CAT worked his way into our lives. He and Yazzie reached a sort of detente. They were never buddies exactly, but in recent years they seemed to tolerate each other. If one was asleep in the TV room, the other was snoozing nearby.

I got over my allergy, or maybe I just accommodated the discomfort because CAT and I got to be pals. We had an evening ritual. He would crawl up on my lap after dinner, and I would tell him a story.

Crazy, isn't it? Telling a cat a story. But I did and he loved it. He looked me right in the eyes and acted as though he understood every word of those nutty stories.

I know cats can't be hypochondriacs, but CAT did seem to have an assortment of mood swings that appeared to be related to his real and imagined ailments. He was diabetic, would occasionally lose patches of hair on his rear end and, in recent years, he developed a heart murmur. Like most big, orange cats, he'd mix it up with other neighborhood cats. Kept himself neat and clean, though.

CAT and I had a great time last weekend. I was taking down the outside Christmas lights, and he got to playing with the extension cords. Gee, he had fun! He'd romp around with those wires while I coiled them up. "You know, for an old guy," I told him, "you really have some great moves."

I suppose you have guessed where I am going with all this. I let him out of the house early Wednesday evening. I called him several times an hour later. "CAT! CAT!" I hollered. But he didn't run up to the front door the way he usually did.

Trish thought she heard him in one of those duets he used to have with the black cat down the street. I got up in the night to try to find him. And we all looked up and down the block Thursday morning, the day I am writing this. There was no trace.

Trish called about an hour ago. She was crying. She had found CAT and he was dead. Trish tried to tell me he was all bloody and had probably frozen to death. "Maybe I could have saved him when I heard him last night," she sobbed.

CAT's death is tough on all of us, but particularly Trish. She was the one who always patched him up after his nocturnal skirmishes and took him to Anderson when he needed veterinarian care. She really gave him the personality he developed over the years.

I guess I'm not handling CAT's death very well, either. I really don't know what I'll do tonight when it is storytime.

January 6, 1985

9

WARS AND PEACE

Always remember men of November

Doughboys.

Nov. 11 is Armistice Day. There are some American traditions with which there should be no tampering. Armistice Day is one of them. We need this day to restore dignity and meaning to the words "Lest we forget."

But we have forgotten. We don't remember the stench of the Somme and Passchendaele battlefields. Gone is the horror of American bodies stacked at Belleau Wood and Chateau Thierry. The agony of Verdun has even slipped from the memories of most French and German citizens. The 9 million people slaughtered in the Great War have become little more than statistical footnotes in history books.

Since the 11th hour of the 11th day of the 11th month in 1918, we have had World War II, the Korean War and Vietnam. And for reasons of convenience, we have lumped the honoring of all surviving veterans into an all-purpose, generic Veterans Day. We trivialize their sacrifices by just giving government workers a day off on Monday.

There is only the minor inconvenience of having no mail delivery, offset by not being required to feed parking meters. Even that great American crapshoot, the New York Stock Exchange, will be open as usual.

The three-day weekend does little to remind us that we are living in the most barbarous century in history. It isn't the "red badge of courage" we'll honor this weekend, but the red-tag sales on microwave ovens.

Opinion polls show most Americans believe a third global war is inevitable. President Reagan talks easily and philosophically of Armageddon, the final and conclusive battle between good, as represented by the United States, and evil, as represented by the Soviet Union.

That's the problem. We look at war in the abstract. Our leadership sees it, as did Carl von Clausewitz, as "a continuation of policy by other means." It is tragically true that most world leaders who think of war in those terms, and believe it to be survivable and winable, have never been to war.

191

For most Americans, war is something that happens to other people, in other places, at other times. But to those who have actually stood up to "the red animal — war, the blood-swollen god," as Stephen Crane wrote, the idea of another world conflict is intolerable, unimaginable.

That is why Nov. 11 will always be Armistice Day to me, not just Veterans Day. I want to remember the doughboys in their wrapped puttees as they faced the great death. I want to hear them sing about the Mademoiselle from Armentieres who "hasn't been kissed in 40 years."

I want the world to remember how they struggled in skirmish lines through clouds of mustard gas, how they lived in slime, and how endless cannonades shattered their minds and mangled their bodies. I want us somehow to feel, as they did, a quavering fear in the guts when the captain commanded, "Fix bayonets!"

Armistice Day was the day when all the madness stopped, and peace and quiet returned to Earth for a precious split second in eternity. It is a time worth remembering.

Lest we forget.

November 11, 1984

Day to remember our quiet war

FORGOTTEN.

June 25 marks the 35th anniversary of the beginning of the war no one wants to remember. Even though casualties on both sides exceeded 3.5 million, it was a war that ended in an armistice, not a peace treaty.

There is no national monument honoring its veterans. Few books have been written about it. It was a war that stopped where it began. It was a war we didn't even call a war.

But the Korean War was a war by any measurement, not the "police action," as political leaders characterized it. America has been so busy indulging itself in self-pity and guilt over Vietnam that it has forgotten the sacrifices Americans made in Korea.

Unlike the Vietnam War, the war in Korea had no Jane Fonda and was not televised. But by strange irony, most young Americans know about the Korean War only by what they have seen on "M*A*S*H," the TV series about doctors and nurses in a Mobile Army Surgical Hospital.

While occasional gratuitous anti-war sentiment surfaced in "M*A*S*H" scripts, the program played the war mostly for laughs. Ask most Americans what they remember about the series and answers would certainly involve the corporal in drag, irreverent surgeons who drank martinis, the clerk who slept with a teddy bear and the colonel who was devoted to his horse.

North Koreans were usually portrayed as poor, misunderstood peasants, either victims of circumstance or comic figures. In none of the scripts were they depicted as the drum-beating, cymbal-pounding, obscenity-screaming, ruthless thugs they really were.

Enemy troops are rarely nice guys, I suppose. But in my experience in two wars, I have never seen soldiers as brutal, as savage or as unprincipled as the North Koreans.

It all began June 25, 1950, at 4 a.m. when the North Korean army attacked without warning across the 38th parallel boundary between North and South Korea. There were only 500 American military advisers in the country. Before it was over, more than 50,000 Americans had been killed. In addition to U.S. forces, token troops from 22 other countries participated in the United Nations defense of South Korea.

America remembers the Korean War because it provided the reason President Harry Truman fired Gen. Douglas MacArthur for insubordination.

I remember it for America's infantry soldiers. They fought bravely and well despite lack of support at home and an unfair Selective Service system that favored the well-to-do at the expense of the poor. Truman integrated the armed forces just before the Korean War. Until then, units were all black or all white, but never mixed.

With all of the delayed reaction to the Vietnam War we have seen lately, and the 40th anniversary of the end of World War II, it is sad Americans can't find room in their memories for those who fought and died in that nasty little war that wasn't a war.

Quote: *We fight all day long, and we drink all night through. That's how brave men are dying for bastards like you.* — GI song about swivel-chair colonels.

June 25, 1985

The real M*A*S*H

SOMEWHERE IN KOREA — OUR LAST BROADCAST FROM THE KOREAN WAR-front came from an Air Force medical evacuation plane. The voices of the men you heard were wounded a few hours earlier. All of them had been carried by litter down the steep mountain slopes or evacuated by helicopter to battalion aid stations. From there they were taken by Army ambulance to a Medical Corps clearing station and then to this Mobile Army Surgical Hospital.

It is a rambling affair on a muddy, crowded side street of this small Korean town. Across the street from the entrance is a row of ramshackle huts that serve as stores. A sign over one of them reads: "Welcome U-N Forces. Develop And Print Picture." Another says: "Star Laundr. Make Good Wash And Repair." An endless stream of Korean and American humanity competes with honking military vehicles for space along this muddy street. A Korean MP toots his whistle constantly and waves his dirty white gloves at the traffic. No one pays any attention to him.

There is a small guardhouse at the hospital gate. The sign over the door says: "There will be no drinking or loafing on this post by order of the Provost Marshal." A dirty Korean boy in dirtier green Army fatigues sleeps peacefully under the sign. Vans, ambulances and buses are shuttling the wounded from the airstrip. Like all Korean roads, this one is marked with ruts and chuckholes. The vehicles are moving slowly, but at each jolt the wounded moan and gasp at the pain.

Finally, the convoy comes to a halt in front of the admission room, a low Army-built Butler hut. Immediately, teams of volunteer British, Australian and New Zealand litter bearers open ambulance doors and begin to carry out the filthy, unshaven, wounded men. Inside the hut, the litters are placed on the floor. The men are then checked by a Medical Corps triage sergeant who looks at their green EMTs — Emergency Medical Tag — attached to each patient's dog tags or uniform.

He checks to see which of the men are in critical condition. They get treatment first. The less seriously wounded wait a little longer. The ones who have died en route are processed last. They are moved to the side of the room where Graves Registration soldiers identify them by their dog tags and cut out their pockets for personal possessions to be mailed home. Pornographic pictures, if any, are pulled out.

The patients are then carried to a secondary admitting room. Three exhausted medical officers check each patient's wounds to determine where they will be sent next. In the same room, five Korean workers in dirty white peasant garb are hammering strips of brown linoleum over the greasy floor boards. Patients requiring X-rays are taken across the room where three medics, stripped to the waist, lift them gingerly off the litters and onto the X-ray table. One patient — he must be 6 foot 4 — had been badly mangled by mortar fragments. The attendants ripped his blood-drenched shorts from his otherwise naked body. Just as the X-ray was about to be taken, the big man half awakened from his morphine-induced sleep, groaned fitfully and tried to get up. The attendants finally pushed and talked him back into place and the X-ray was taken.

The laboratory is in the opposite corner of the room. Two corporals and one sergeant are squinting into microscopes. There is a pinup picture of a nude woman on a shelf holding bottles and test tubes. Next to it is a small bouquet of flowers in an old pickle jar. The flowers seem out of place. But what is a hospital without flowers?

Now we walk out of the big admitting room through a covered corridor into the surgery building. It is another one of those long Butler huts. A hallway runs down the center of the building. Supply rooms and sterilizing equipment are on the left. On the right are five operating rooms. But they are not rooms at all; they are just cubicles divided by mosquito netting with two operating tables in each cubicle. There is a hooded light over each table. It is possible to stand at one end of the hall and watch 10 operations at once through the eerie green light created by the mosquito netting. The effect is surreal.

A radio at the end of the hall is playing a Dave Rose recording of "Dancing in the Dark." A voice says, "I can't understand it. We're not supposed to be doing anything at the front, but we are getting casualties like mad."

Now it's a Peggy Lee record on the radio. "Why don't you do right like the other men do," she sings. The hard edge of a nurse's voice interrupts: "Take this guy outta here and put him in a ward. Make it snappy!"

At the next table, the surgeon grabs a wad of cotton in the jaws of a hemostat. He pours a yellowish-pink liquid over it and begins to swab out a 2-inch hole in what was once a man's hand. The patient is under anesthetic and can't hear the doctor say: "You know what, George?

This is my wedding anniversary. Whatta place to spend a wedding anniversary."

In the next cubicle, a man's throat lies open. Two nurses put clamps on the skin to hold it back while the surgeon works. A Ralph Flanagan recording is now playing on the radio. "That new lieutenant colonel acts like a bum. Anti-social. Won't talk to anyone," says a nurse in her late 30s.

A small Korean boy dressed in a dirty surgical gown is sweeping the floor. "No, no boy-san! Hava-no taksan water! Hava-yes skoshee water! Understand?" a nurse shouts at him as a doctor dressed in a red rubber apron goes from cubicle to cubicle. He is wearing a white cap on the back of his head and there is a stethoscope hanging out of his hip pocket. A short cigarette with a long ash dangles from the corner of his mouth.

All the doctors and nurses look tired. They should be. I learned later they had handled 700 acute battle casualties in this room in 72 hours.

Two litter bearers enter one of the cubicles where an unconscious Marine has just had mortar fragments removed from his leg. "Wake up, Mac," one of them says as he slaps the Marine's face. "Snap out of it. Let's get his ass on the litter and get him outta here. Somebody grab the net and hold it open."

Two doctors pass in the narrow hall. One of them says, "Hey, Fred, don't forget we got an amputation at 8."

Amputation at 8, I think to myself. *Dinner at 7, in the sack by 9. Up at 5 in the morning, breakfast at 6, and here they come again. Wounded and more wounded. Sick and more sick.*

The whole scene becomes almost a hallucination. The stream of casualties has no end. *Dust, mud, cold, heat, flies, mosquitos, nurses who think lieutenant colonels are anti-social, blood off the floor, dead flesh off the hand, body odor, ether, garlic, dirty sheets and no sheets at all, goldbricks, heroes, bourbon from Japan, rotation, no rotation, dog tags, piles of muddy combat boots, a nosy correspondent, flowers in the lab, VD and more VD.*

There are sounds, too. Close-support Sabre jets roar overhead. And then there is the radio that is always on, the moaning and screaming of the wounded, the shouting of the litter bearers. Listen to the voices of the men and women who are trying to paste shattered lives back together:

"I'm a pediatrician. What the hell am I doing here?"

"I wonder how Lucy is. Seven months over here is too goddamn long."

"That ain't no accident. He shot himself in the foot to get off the line. I'd like to slug him. Bastard."

"These fatigues don't fit."

"Jordan says he is a surgical tech. Hell, he doesn't know a hemostat from a sledgehammer."

And so it goes.

"You a correspondent? Let me tell you a war story, Mac," a voice says from the adjoining ward. "Here's where the bullet went in," he says pointing to a bandage on his chest. "And here is where it went out my back. I got hit three days ago and I been walking all over this place since yesterday. The chow is great. Pal, I got me a million-dollar wound. I think I'm gonna get to go home. That gook bullet just missed my heart and chipped a bone. I shaved myself this morning."

End of war story.

But when will the war end? No one knows. If they think about it here in this Mobile Army Surgical Hospital, they don't talk about it. The talk is of little things, and there is little time for that as the convoys of wounded line up before the gate.

From a broadcast on the Columbine Radio Network, Summer 1951.

War scene drenched in red

SEOUL, SOUTH KOREA — THIS IS SEOUL. WE HAVE JUST TAKEN IT AGAIN. ONE-and-one-half million people lived here. Now, Seoul is a ghost city that was once three times the size of Denver. Imagine the desolation if you can. Add to it the rotten smells and wind-whipped powdered dust.

A murderous sun shines down on what's left of fire-blackened buildings, pitted by random machine-gun fire. Swarms of flies are everywhere. Dazed refugees pick their way through a jungle of telephone poles at crazy angles and tramway wires snapping in the wind. A 5-year-old beggar orphan tugs at your sleeve with one hand and scratches open sores on his leg with his other.

That roaring sound you hear is a column of 6-by-6, 2½-ton trucks bringing supplies from Taegu to the front. Over the main road is a limp banner that says "Welcome U.N. Forces." It is rarely more than a few minutes until a flight of fighter-bomber jets roars overhead to join the infantry in a close-support mission.

But maybe you have seen it all before at Frankfurt, Berlin, Aachen, Cologne, Warsaw, St. Lo, Vienna, Wonsan or Hungnam. Just three years ago it might have been Jerusalem of Jaffa. Those who lived in Washington, D.C., during the War of 1812 saw it. Rome burned, too. Athens was once destroyed. And now it is Seoul. What city is next? The world learns little and remembers nothing.

Last night I drove my Jeep through here at dusk. I had been with the Greek battalion attached to the 7th Cavalry Regiment. Just as I nosed it over the last hill overlooking the city, the full terror of this vicious little war seemed to envelop me.

In the west, the sun was just sinking from sight. By any standards but these, it would have been beautiful. Rays of blood-red light punctured the thin layers of mist and clouds of dust. The shattered buildings, the naked walls, the cratered streets: They all reflected the glow. Everything was as red as blood. Or was it fire? I looked at my hands. They were red, too.

If captured in a split second, what I saw could have been an artist's conception of hell. Maybe it is hell and those of us imprisoned here are too foolish not to know it.

From a broadcast on the Columbine Radio Network, Spring 1951.

GI found a home far from home

IT HAD BEEN A LONG, JOLTING 400-MILE RIDE IN THE BACK OF A 2½-TON, 6-by-6 truck from Mittweida, Germany, to Vervier, Belgium. Bridges along the autobahn had been destroyed, forcing us to travel along shell-cratered side roads. We were butt-sore and dusty when transferred to boxcars for the rail trip through Paris to Le Havre. I had lost track of the date, but it must have been during the last week of April 1945.

The war in Europe was all but over for the 6th Armored Division. We had crossed the Mulde River at Rochlitz and the Zachopau River at Mittweida. We could have gone on and taken Dresden, crossed the Elbe River and advanced unopposed into Czechoslovakia, but we were ordered to halt and wait for the historic linkup with the Russian army.

All that was a jumble in my mind as the train clattered west toward Paris. I looked down at my rifle on the splintered floor of the boxcar and realized that for the first time since we rolled off the landing craft onto Utah Beach in Normandy an eternity earlier, it was not loaded.

It didn't matter because I was on my way to England. I couldn't believe my good luck. Only 20 of more than 10,000 GIs in the 6th had been selected to take a two-week furlough in Europe and I was one of them. I wanted to go to England because we had been stationed there the year before the invasion.

When the captain told me about the furlough, I was digging a garbage pit.

To this day, I don't know why I was chosen. It certainly wasn't because of any personal heroism or valuable service on my part. But at that point, I didn't care. Behind me were five European Theater of Operations campaigns: Normandy, Northern France, Ardennes, Rhineland and Central Europe.

As the boxcar swayed back and forth, I closed my eyes and tried to blot out memories of bloated corpses, smashed villages, sobbing women, frightened children and endless lines of refugees. There would be no more killing, no more screaming German 88mm shells, no more enemy "Bedcheck Charlie" planes, no more mud, no more cold, no more slit trenches, no more death camps and no more splats of blue flame in pre-dawn darkness from fish-tail exhausts of Sherman tanks.

The freight train was taking us away from all that. It wouldn't be stopping at Leipzig, Buchenwald, Weimar, Erfurt, Muhlhausen in Thuringen, Kassel, Bad Nauheim, Worms, Rhein-Durkheim, Frankfurt, the Siegfried Line, Bastogne, Metz, Nancy, Lorient, Brest, Avranches, St. Lo or at any of the other battlegrounds we had survived in Gen. George S. Patton's 3rd Army along the way.

As recently as a week earlier, we had been in a savage firefight along the Zeitz-Leipzig line. In a fanatic, last-ditch assault, 1,500 German troops made a suicide attack against our advance guard. We destroyed them. In the final days before we were ordered to halt our advance, we "smoked," or burned to the ground with white phosphorous shells, every village, every hamlet where there was the slightest opposition to our patrols or where there wasn't a white surrender flag in every window. It was *our* "final solution."

A great quiet had descended on the front. We could smell the moistness of spring in the air, and we could hear birds and watch fields become a pale green. For us, the Great War had finally ended. Like a tired and scarred old beast, our division slumped to the ground

and began to rest and to lick its wounds. It was then and there my odyssey to London and V-E Day began.

There were two other soldiers in the boxcar from the 6th: Capt.
Joseph Kruchanski, a Roman Catholic chaplain, and Staff Sgt. Thomas O'Sullivan, a cavalry platoon sergeant. I had known "Father Joe,"
as we called him, because he had filled in at our outfit after our
chaplain's legs had been blown off when he stepped on a mine while
trying to save a wounded soldier.

Everyone liked Father Joe. He talked straight, was a two-fisted
cognac drinker and he was a relentless draw poker player. I had not
seen much of him since Christmas Eve at Tentelingen, Germany, the
night before we were ordered from the Saar River to Belgium and
what would be remembered as the Battle of the Bulge.

"Jesus Christ," he whispered as he threw down his cards in a
candle-lighted farmhouse. "What time is it? I gotta go say Christmas
Mass for the 44th Infantry."

O'Sullivan was a soft-spoken recon trooper who had served his
time as point man on countless combat command and combat team
operations. He had been with the 6th since Day One.

I suppose we all stank to high heaven. I hadn't had my uniform off
in more than a month, the last time I had the nominal wash-up that
GIs called a "whore's bath." It had been almost a year since my last
professional haircut. Father Joe and O'Sullivan were in about the
same condition.

No one seemed to notice the odor. After a while, everyone gets to
stinking the same, and pretty soon stink is stink and no one smells it
anymore. That's the way it was with us in that old French boxcar.

All that changed in the reception center at Le Havre. "I want all
you men to strip to the skin and stow all of your gear including your
helmets and weapons in a duffel bag," we were told by an immacu-
late warrant officer. "Take showers in the next room and then move
to the equipment area where you will be fitted with new Winter 'A'
uniforms.

"Your unit insignia and stripes will be sewn on for you by French
nationals. You will be issued extra socks, underwear and shirts and
new shaving equipment and other toilet articles. After you are
dressed, move to the next building where you will be given haircuts.
We want you to look like garrison soldiers when you get to England."

I never wanted to leave that hot shower. The pinpoints of scalding
water between my shoulder blades washed away fatigue and pain. As
the filth of four nations swirled down the drain at my feet, I didn't
care if we ever got to England. This was furlough enough for me. I

stayed under the shower until the tips of my fingers shriveled.

A couple of hours later it didn't appear as though I had ever had a bad day. I looked at the reflection of the GI in the full-length mirror. I hardly recognized him. From his new haircut down to his shined combat boots, Cpl. Frank E. Amole Jr., 37342310, was a 22-year-old soldier boy any mother would be proud to call son. And he didn't stink. Not even a little bit.

That's the way Father Joe, O'Sullivan and I looked when the channel boat put in at Southampton — the same Southampton where we had embarked almost a year earlier for Normandy. There were V-2 rockets and buzz bombs in the sky then, but on the day we returned to England there were only white puffs of clouds.

On the train to London, we decided to stick together even after we had checked in at the Red Cross billet near Regent Street. Father Joe didn't seem like an officer, even though he was wearing a dress tunic and captain's bars. He was more like us. He had a bottle of Hennessy's in his musette bag and we each had a "pull" or two on the train.

It was May 1 when we got to London. The last time I had been there was shortly after we had arrived in England from the United States. I was on a 36-hour pass then and got there just in time for the heaviest nighttime German air raid on London of the war.

It was different this time. The singsong air raid sirens were silent, but there were still a few barrage balloons lazing over the outskirts of the city. Vast sections of London were shattered, but I spotted a few clumps of buttercups sprouting from some of the mounds of rubble.

I felt strangely disoriented as I walked through the crowds the first few days. I kept bumping into people and apologizing for my clumsiness. Sometimes I had to sit down to get my bearings when things seemed to be closing in on me. Father Joe and O'Sullivan were having the same problems. We just weren't accustomed to being around people. It is one thing to slosh in the mud alone and quite another to navigate through hurrying pedestrians on the crowded Strand.

We decided to meet each morning at 11 at Rainbow Corner and try to return to Germany together when our Cinderella furloughs had ended. O'Sullivan had never been to London and wanted to see the sights. Father Joe had his own agenda, and somehow I had the feeling it didn't involve visiting holy places.

At first I slept a lot and tried to get my "city legs." Then I decided to have my picture taken for my parents to reassure them I was all right. There had been a period of weeks when I hadn't written home at all.

As we plodded through the winter, I had become despondent. I felt helpless, inundated by the death and massive destruction that was everywhere. It had become impossible for us to be just observers of the spectacle. We had been drawn into its vastness, its brutality, its insanity.

Life had become just existence. Sometimes I didn't really believe we would make it. The end of the war seemed so distant. I stopped writing home simply because I had nothing to say. I could no longer relate to what it must have been like back in the States. I didn't feel as though I was a part of that life anymore. For me, it was just one bleak, pointless day after another.

My parents were terrified when the letters stopped. They didn't know whether I was alive or dead. Of the eight boys who had gone to war from my old neighborhood, five had been killed. And so my mother finally wrote to my commanding officer.

He showed me her letter and told me I had by-God-better write to her or he would have my ass "and all its fixtures," as he put it. "I got other things to do beside play post office with everybody's mother."

I didn't have to go far to find a photo studio. I just happened to stumble upon Mayfair Portraits, 25 Piccadilly, London, W.1., not far from the Red Cross billets. I explained to the young woman behind the counter what I wanted and asked her to mail the photograph to my parents. "Of course we can do that," she replied, "if you trust me to choose from one of the proofs."

After the photograph was taken, I paid her and left the studio. I hadn't gone more than a couple of blocks when I realized I wanted to know her better. It could have been that clean, fresh-scrubbed aroma about her, or the nice way she looked at me, or both. I turned around and went back to the studio.

"Yes?" she said when I came back through the door. "Would there be something else?"

I felt like such a sap. It had been a year since I had spoken to, or even been around, a woman. I wanted so much for her to approve of me, but I was flustered and could feel my face flushing. I tried looking down at my feet to regain what little composure I had. I started several times to mumble something about going out with me after she got off work. It was so awkward. I shuffled my boots and then clasped my hands behind my back and squared my shoulders as though ordered by some unseen platoon sergeant to stand at parade rest.

I was about ready to break and run when she smiled and said, "Look, I'll be off work at 5. Why don't you come back then and we'll walk about some and have tea. Then you can see me home."

I wondered if she could hear my heart pounding and if my face was as red as it felt. My mouth was dry and I was a little dizzy. *God,* I thought, *What will we talk about? I don't know anything to talk about.*

I began to relax after I met her and we strolled around for awhile. Her name was Dorothy Fuller. She lived with her parents, Mr. and Mrs. D.W. Fuller, in a little house at 13 Foxbourne Road, Balham, in Kennington. Her brother was in the British Army and her fiance had been a Royal Air Force bomber pilot until he was shot down and killed over Belgium. I learned later it was on his last scheduled mission. A date had been set for the wedding.

The Fullers were active in civil defense. Everyone in London was. Dorothy and her mother had been plane spotters, air raid wardens and hospital nurses' aides. They didn't complain, but it was clear that their war, in a different way, had been as rough as mine. In the years since, each time I see scratchy black-and-white newsreel film of the Battle of Britain, I think of the Fullers and the other Londoners who endured so much for so long.

Dorothy was slim and quite fair. Her hair was a pale copper color and her eyes were a deep blue. She was not beautiful or glamorous by movie star standards, but she was quite pretty, and there was a look of kindness and gentleness around her mouth. As we rode the underground toward Balham Station, I sensed a quiet dignity about her.

When we walked up to her door, she asked me to come in to meet her parents. They were very gracious. I felt like an oaf again. My awkwardness and clumsiness came back, and so did my red face. I hated myself for letting my face get red. I was terrified I would lapse into GI talk, which consisted mainly of four-letter profanity.

Before I left to return to the Red Cross billet, Dorothy and I made plans to attend a play the following evening after she was off work. She told me she would get the tickets and we'd have something to eat at the Criterion restaurant near where the statue of Eros had stood on Oxford Circus. I was so dumb I didn't know Eros was the Greek god of love. Maybe she didn't know it, either.

The play was a comedy, but it probably wasn't as funny as I must have appeared between acts when we were served tea at our seats as is the custom in London. I spilled the tea trying to hold the tray at the same time I was fumbling for my billfold to pay the 10-bob check.

Dorothy was very patient with me and helped smooth over my slapstick performance.

When I took her home, her mother was waiting for us at the door. She invited me in and said, "Gene — can I call you that? — Mr. Fuller and I have talked it over, and we would be pleased to have you remain with us in our home for the rest of your leave. Spend the night. You can pick up your things at the Red Cross tomorrow. Come upstairs, let me show you where you will stay."

Dorothy managed an embarrassed little smile. I thought her face seemed a bit flushed, too. Mrs. Fuller led us to the top of the stairs and through an open door. "This is our son John's room," she said, turning her head away. Her voice caught for a second. "It is just as it was before he went off to service. Do think of it as your home-away-from-home. The bed is quite comfortable."

Mrs. Fuller turned and left. Dorothy and I said goodnight. She reached over and squeezed my hand. I closed the door and sat for a moment on the chair by the small desk. Suddenly, I was over-whelmed by their kindness and began to cry. I couldn't remember the last time I had cried about anything. The tragedy of the war seemed to well up in my chest all at once. It was terrible, and yet what was happening to me in that home was so wonderful. I couldn't seem to sort it all out.

Exhausted, I undressed and slipped between the cool, cotton sheets of the feather bed. It was so marvelously soft. Within seconds, I must have fallen into a deep, dreamless sleep. No one would awaken me for guard duty in the middle of that night. No mortars would shatter the blessed quiet of that room. The ground under the Fullers' modest home would not shudder under the tracks of thousands of tanks.

The next thing I knew someone had kissed me. It was morning. I opened my eyes and there was Dorothy standing beside my bed. There was that fresh, well-scrubbed aroma again. She was smiling and holding a tray with a pot of tea and some cakes. "This is the way we awaken loved ones in England," she said. "After you finish your tea, I'll bring you breakfast. And then we'll go into the city. The war is officially over. The king is going on the BBC at 7 o'clock. This is Victory Day, and we're going to celebrate."

May 8. V-E Day. Victory in Europe Day. If there was a single place in the world to be on V-E Day it was London, where so many civilians had endured Germany's devastating air attacks.

When Winston Churchill described the Battle of Britain as "an ordeal of the most grievous kind," he offered the English people nothing but "blood, toil, tears and sweat." And in his first speech as prime minister, he asked: "What is our aim? I can answer it in one word: victory."

The Battle of Britain began when France fell. "The infantry that bore the brunt of this new type of warfare," John Dos Passos would later write, "were the air-raid wardens and the men who ran about the roofs of London putting out incendiary bombs and the weary squads that dug out people buried under crumpled houses."

Londoners drew great strength from Churchill's firm voice on the BBC. "Let us therefore brace ourselves to our duties, and so bear ourselves that, if the British Empire and its Commonwealth last for a thousand years, men will say: 'This was their finest hour.' "

Surely it had been the Fuller family's finest hour. This was their day, their special moment in history, and just by pure chance I had become a part of it. Their ordeal was over and so were the "blood, toil, tears and sweat."

Dorothy and I were caught up in that incomparable victory celebration. We were tossed about by the throngs like flotsam on a wild sea. Laughing crowds surged through every street. We saw Irish guardsmen brawling just for the hell of it. We were there when King George, Queen Elizabeth, Princess Elizabeth and Princess Margaret Rose appeared on the balcony of Buckingham Palace.

Drunken journalists were roistering in front of the Fleet Street newspaper plants. Eighth Air Force GIs exploded firecrackers with shortened fuses over the heads of the throngs outside Rainbow Corner. A tipsy member of Parliament made his way along a second-floor ledge in Parliament Square as the crowds cheered him on.

People couldn't wait for the darkness. At long last, there would be no blackout for the first time in years. Every light that could be turned on was turned on. People threw open their windows to let out the light. Searchlights crisscrossed the sky like giant wheel spokes.

How those Londoners loved the light! They wanted to breathe it, bathe in it, cover everything with it. There was light everywhere. Light had become their symbol of liberation, of freedom, of victory! There was a popular song during the war that began, "When the lights go on again all over the world." Well, they were on that joyous night in London town.

At about three o'clock in the morning, Dorothy and I began to make our way back to Balham. I noticed a strange, sad thing as the celebration began to wind down. People were again drawing blackout curtains across their windows. "It will take a long time to break the habit," Dorothy explained.

When we finally sat down in the subway coach, Dorothy put her head on my shoulder and went to sleep. She was at complete peace with the world, and so was I. The war was over.

May 5, 1985

EPILOGUE.

The next few days were quiet. All England was savoring the peace. Dorothy and I walked her old dog, Sam, through the small green common near her home each evening. Sometimes we'd see a film, ending each day quietly, often just listening to the radio or talking with her parents in the living room of the little house at 13 Foxbourne Road.

Father Joe, O'Sullivan and I met each morning at Rainbow Corner. The $165 I had borrowed was running low. Our furlough time had ended and we were officially absent without leave. We weren't too worried about that since transportation between England and France was uncertain because of V-E Day.

Even so, we knew we had to go back soon. None of us wanted to let go of the time we had spent in London. We wanted somehow to keep the spirit of V-E Day forever. I certainly didn't want to leave Dorothy and my "home-away-from-home" with the Fullers.

When the day came, I packed my gear and said goodbye to Mr. and Mrs. Fuller. There was no way I could adequately thank them for taking me in. I later learned that Dorothy served me breakfast in bed every morning because I was getting the family's entire food ration of eggs, meat, kippers, fruit and milk. They didn't want me to know that or see what they were eating for breakfast.

Dorothy got off work and went with me to Waterloo Station on the underground. We didn't talk much on the way. She was wearing my little gold signet ring I had given her the night before. The gold locket she gave me was in the pocket of the small leather picture frame with her photograph I was carrying in my Ike jacket pocket. She had inscribed it "To sweet Gene."

The scene at Waterloo could have come from any wartime motion picture of the period. Young and old people were seeing off men in uniform, only this time the men were going off to peace, not to war.

I watched Dorothy out of the coach window as long as I could as the train pulled out of the station. It was the last time I would ever see her. I sat down with Father Joe and O'Sullivan. We rode in silence, each of us keeping his memories, his hopes and his regrets to himself.

When the channel boat docked at Le Havre, we returned to the reception center. We felt as though we were re-entering a kind of time tunnel. We turned in our clean, new uniforms for the reeking combat gear we had worn before. It was back in the boxcar the next day and off for Paris.

It was there we decided not to be herded like sheep anymore. "What the hell, we're AWOL anyhow," O'Sullivan reasoned.

Since the chances were remote we would ever see Paris again, we jumped out of the boxcar and made our way into the city. We shambled our way from one end of the Champs-Elysees to the other. We watched the action at Pig Alley (Place Pigalle). We went to the top of Montmartre where we marched ceremoniously, if somewhat unsteadily, through Mere Catherine's bistro to the stirring off-key music of a pickup military band made up of ancient French war veterans in ancient French uniforms.

We slept under Pont Neuf, the bridge that crosses the Seine at Ile de la Cite. We scrounged food from reppledepples (replacement centers) and tried to stay out of the way of the increasing number of "snowdrops." They were the military policemen wearing white helmets and white leggings that seemed to be running Paris in those wild days after the war. I did learn one thing by the experience: If you are ever going over-the-hill, manage to stay close to a chaplain. Silver bars and silver cross insignia discourage embarrassing questions.

When we finally found the 6th, it was withdrawing west of Leipzig. The Russians were gradually taking over East Germany. My battalion was bivouacked near Kranichfeld, a village 12 miles south of Weimar. "Where the hell have you been?" the CO thundered as I reported in.

"I was with Father Joe," I mumbled.

"I didn't ask you who you were with. I want to know where you were!"

"We had some problems getting out of Paris." I was whispering by then.

"A lot of people are having problems getting out of Paris. Tear off those stripes. NOW!" he shouted.

Feeling something like a dime-novel Alfred Dreyfus, I fumbled around and finally tore off my corporal's stripes.

Then the "old man" — actually, he was only 30 — began to laugh. "You were promoted to buck sergeant while you were gone."

The days before we could go home grew into weeks and then into months. The 6th had fallen back to Frankfurt by the time the Potsdam Conference began in midsummer. President Franklin D. Roosevelt had died just before the war ended, Winston Churchill had been replaced in an election as prime minister by Clement Attlee.

Our outfit was chosen to be the honor guard for President Truman, Attlee and Gen. Dwight D. Eisenhower. We were lined up on either side of the highway in front of our vehicles. Our battered old tanks, M-7s and halftracks had been smeared with motor oil to make them appear shiny. Soldiers from Missouri were placed in the front ranks so that Truman could talk to them if he stopped.

He didn't. Their open limousine was just a blur when they sped by. I don't think they even looked at us or our oily vehicles. I do know it took days to clean them up. What we didn't know was that the Potsdam Conference was really the beginning of a new war, the Cold War.

Just as I came to believe our war was really over, I was transferred to the 3rd "Spearhead" Armored Division, then scheduled to fight the Japanese under Patton in Manchuria. But after Hiroshima and V-J Day in August, I was assigned to a separate battalion where I became sergeant major. Finally, finally, finally, I got back to Denver in late September 1945. I was discharged at Fort Logan a few days later.

Dorothy and I continued to correspond, as did our mothers, but the time between letters lengthened, and then we stopped writing. Her last letter to me was postmarked at Tooting Station, Jan. 14, 1946.

I suppose I had become preoccupied with myself. I wanted to put the war behind me. I was afraid I wouldn't get back my $27.50-a-week radio announcing job. There were old buddies to find. And I was trying to get a handle on my residual "battle rattle" problems. The sound of explosions — even thunder — terrorized and humiliated me, sometimes sending me to cower under a table.

Five years later I returned to London. It was May 8, 1950. This time I was there as a reporter. I went immediately to the Mayfair Portrait Studio. When I asked the young woman behind the counter about Dorothy, she looked up and said, "Are you the Yank?"

When I said I was, she told me that Dorothy and her parents had moved to Hobart, Tasmania, the island state of Australia in the Tasman Sea. She had left no forwarding address.

I spent V-E Day, 1950, alone in London.

Two wars and many years later, my life has certainly changed. I am devoted to my lovely wife. Three of my four children have grown up and moved away. We have a 16-year-old daughter at home. I have been blessed with more luck, more love and more happiness than I deserve.

But each V-E Day, a part of me returns to London, to Dorothy, to the Fullers and that little house at 13 Foxbourne Road.

What is left? These memories, of course, some faded photographs, a few dried flowers from the Fullers' garden, a tiny locket and a tattered, yellow piece of paper dated June 16, 1945. It is in Dorothy's hand:

In every road there is a little homestead, in every house lives somebody's friend, a heart and vibrant personality upon whom someone, somewhere can depend.

The road is named, the paving stones familiar, the knocker has been touched before.

Memories link with every nook and corner.

There lives a friend and who could wish for more?

Go you in winter when the leaves have fallen, go you in summer when the flowers are fair.

There is the home, the certain someone in it, ready to welcome and to help you there.

May 5, 1985

About the author

AT 62, GENE AMOLE HAS HAD CAREERS IN RADIO, TELEVISION AND NEWSPA-pers, sometimes all at the same time. He has also made side trips into the worlds of film making and magazine writing and publishing. Born in Denver, he was educated in the Denver Public Schools and has spent most of his life in the Mile High City.

In recent years, he has been chosen Journalist of the Year by the Colorado Chapter of the Society of Professional Journalists, Sigma Delta Chi; Columnist of the Year by the Colorado Associated Press; and Broadcaster of the Year by the Colorado Broadcasters Associa-ton. In 1985, he received the Community Service Award from the University of Denver and the Brotherhood/Sisterhood Award from the National Conference of Christians and Jews.

Previous awards include the George Foster Peabody Award for a television program he wrote and narrated; Man of the Year by the Colorado Speech Association; and Educator of the Year by the Colorado Medical Society. He holds honorary doctorates of humane letters from Loretto Heights College and the University of Colorado.

Amole retired from broadcasting in 1983 when he and his partner, Ed Koepke, sold the last of their three radio properties. They had been business partners since 1956.

He has been a columnist for the Rocky Mountain News since 1977. "Morning," a collection of his columns, was published in 1983. He also has ventured into other writing assignments with the News, covering both the Democratic and Republican national conventions in 1984. Amole and his colleague, Suzanne Weiss, have recently formed a team to do in-depth interviews with public figures.

Amole and his wife, Patricia, have lived in the same southwest Denver home for 20 years. Of the four Amole children, Susan still lives at home.